DEVELOPING BRITAIN 1740–1900

The Agrarian, Transport and Industrial Revolutions

Jon Nichol

Basil Blackwell · Oxford

CONTENTS

INTRODUCTION

Developing Britain, 1740-1900 looks at Britain during a time of rapid change. In 1740 most people lived in the country and worked in farming. By 1900 two-thirds of the population lived and worked in towns. The speed of change was so fast from 1740 that historians talk of a number of *revolutions* in agriculture, transport and industry. By 1900 we can see many of the marks of modern Britain—things like the motor car and telephone.

Developing Britain looks at and handles historical *evidence*. In this book are some of the clues the past has left behind. Using them, the reader is encouraged to work out his own ideas about how Britain changed between 1740 and 1900. Some of the passages have been slightly adapted to make them easier to read.

The book is carefully arranged for class, group or individual work. Each subject is self-contained, and provides material for topic work. The questions are roughly graded for difficulty, and give scope for pupils who work at different speeds. They try to make pupils think about the past and build up their own picture of it.

History is made up from *evidence* from the past—a debate between sources. Below is one such clue, **A.** Study the photograph, and then answer these questions:

a The picture is of an iron furnace. When was it first built? When was it rebuilt?
b The furnace made cast iron—about three hundred tons a year. What might it have been used for?
c The world's first iron bridge was built near Coalbrookdale, Shropshire, in 1777-81. Furnace **A** is at Coalbrookdale, where the iron for the bridge was made. Is there any *evidence* to link **A** with the building of the iron bridge?

A

CHANGING BRITAIN, 1740-1900

If in 1740 a flying saucer had visited Britain, what might its spacemen have learned about the country? If they had come back in 1900, how might things have changed? In 1740 they might have hovered over the open fields of a village like **A.** In 1900 the fields looked like **B.** If in 1740 the flying saucer had landed on an open field of village **A,** its crew would have seen a farmer ploughing his land like **C.** In 1900 the great-grandson of the farmer in **C** might have

A

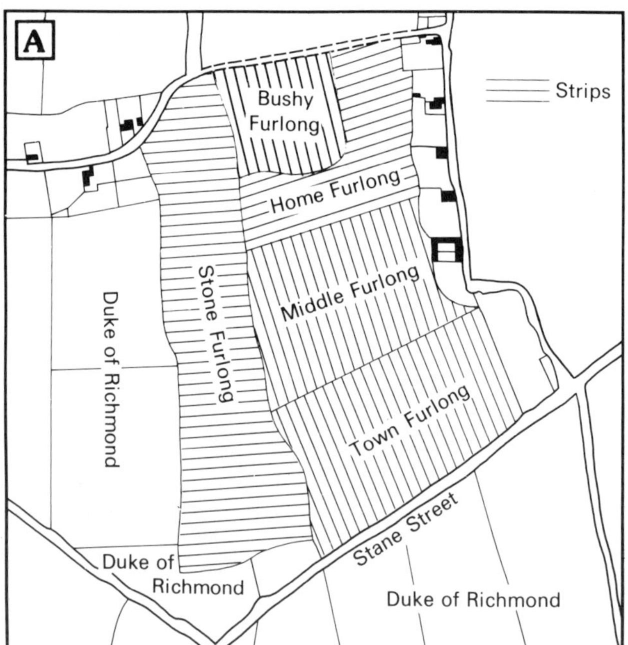

B

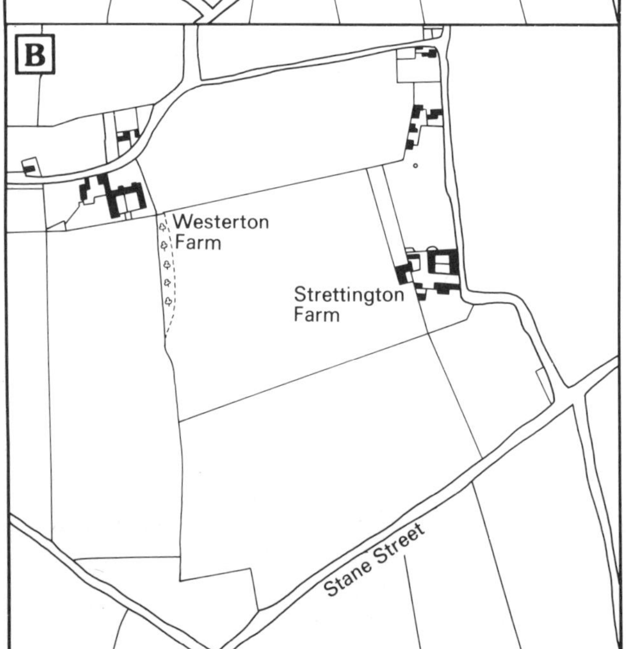

C

D

E **Increase in population in Britain, 1740-1900**

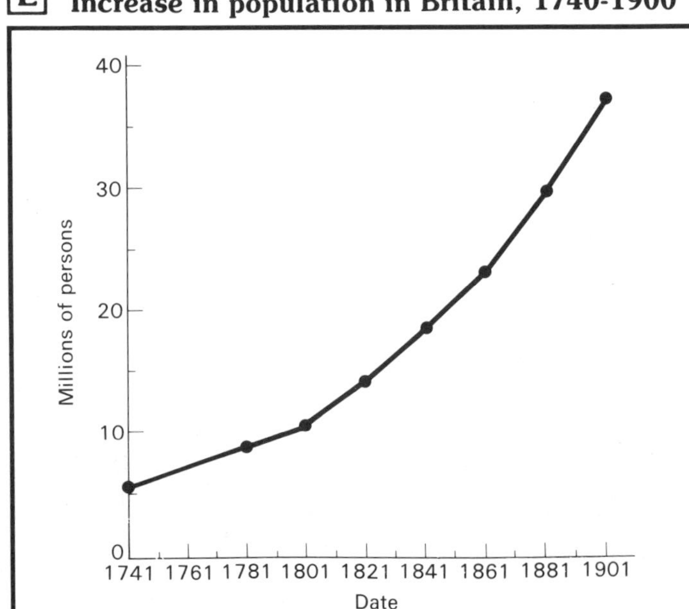

used method **D** to cultivate his land. We call these changes in farming the *Agricultural Revolution.*

The clues **A-D** give some idea of the many changes in Britain from 1740 to 1900. Graph **E** suggests one reason why they happened. The visitors from outer space would have learned that between 1740 and 1900 many new jobs have grown up. **F** shows the main occupations in England and Wales in 1688, 1851 and 1891. In 1851 more people lived in towns and cities than in the country. Most made their livings from working in factories built during the *Industrial Revolution.* By 1900 canals, good roads and a finely spun web of railway lines linked together the villages, towns and cities of Britain. These were built during the *Transport Revolution.*

F	Main Jobs in 1688		Main Jobs in 1851		Main Jobs in 1891	
1	Labourers and servants	1,092,000	Farmworkers	1,790,000	Domestic servants	1,900,000
2	Farmworkers	990,000	Domestic servants	1,039,000	Mining and metal workers	1,503,000
3	Craftsmen	180,000	Textile workers (cotton, silk, linen)	527,000	Farmworkers	1,312,000
4	Seamen	150,000	Building workers	443,000	Textile workers	1,129,000
5	Shopkeepers and traders	120,000	Labourers	376,000	Sewing women	1,100,000
6	Gentlemen (land owners)	36,000	Sewing women	340,000	Transport workers	983,000
7	Merchants	30,000	Wool workers	284,000	House decorators	821,000
8	Clergymen (vicars, priests)	30,000	Shoemakers	274,000	Food and lodgings	798,000
9	Government officials	20,000	Coalminers	219,000	Professions (lawyers, estate agents, etc.)	508,000
10	Lawyers	20,000	Tailors	143,000	Businessmen (factory owners, merchants, traders)	416,000
	Source: Gregory King, an economist who wrote at the time.		*Source:* 1851 Government census		*Source:* Report on the work of the Labour Department of the Board of Trade (1893-94)	

??????????????????????????

1 Choose the right words from the list below the passage to fill in the gaps.

The changes in farming from 1740-1900 are called the ______. One of the many things that changed was how farmers ______ the land. The *Industrial Revolution* meant that many ______ were built. The ______ ______ saw the building of canals, roads and railways.

Transport Revolution, turnips, ploughed, pigsties, factories, Agricultural Revolution

2 The *evidence* on these pages helps you work out some of the ways in which Britain changed between 1740 and 1900. Write out the table below, with your answers under each question.

a What had happened to the fields of area **A** between 1740 and 1900?

b How did the way in which the farmer ploughed his land change from 1740 to 1900?

c Why might the 1900 method be better?

d By how much had the population risen between 1740 and 1900?

e Why do you think this growth happened?

f What jobs do you think people did in 1851 that they did not do in 1688?

g Where did they do this work?

3 Pretend you are meeting one of the spacemen. What might he tell you about how Britain changed between 1740 and 1900?

4 How useful are **A-F** as sources for history?

BACKGROUND TO CHANGE

The *evidence* on pages 4-5 show that there were many changes between 1740 and 1900 in how people farmed, travelled by road, canal or railway, and made goods such as iron. The *agricultural, transport* and *industrial revolutions* still affect our lives—such as where we live and the jobs we do. All around you, you can see *evidence* of how Britain altered after 1740.

To help us understand this change we will use map **A.** It shows an imaginary area in 1740. The map is based on the *actual situation* in parts of Britain. This book looks at how the whole of region **A** changed from 1740-1900. In detail, it looks at what happened in Areas 1, 2, 3 and 4.

The people who lived in the new towns and worked in factories and offices had to eat. Pages 8-9 examine new ways in which farmers grew food and ran their farms during the *agricultural revolution*.

Map **B** shows a village, Blockney, in 1740. How did farming change in this area from 1740-1900?

B **Blockney Village, 1740**

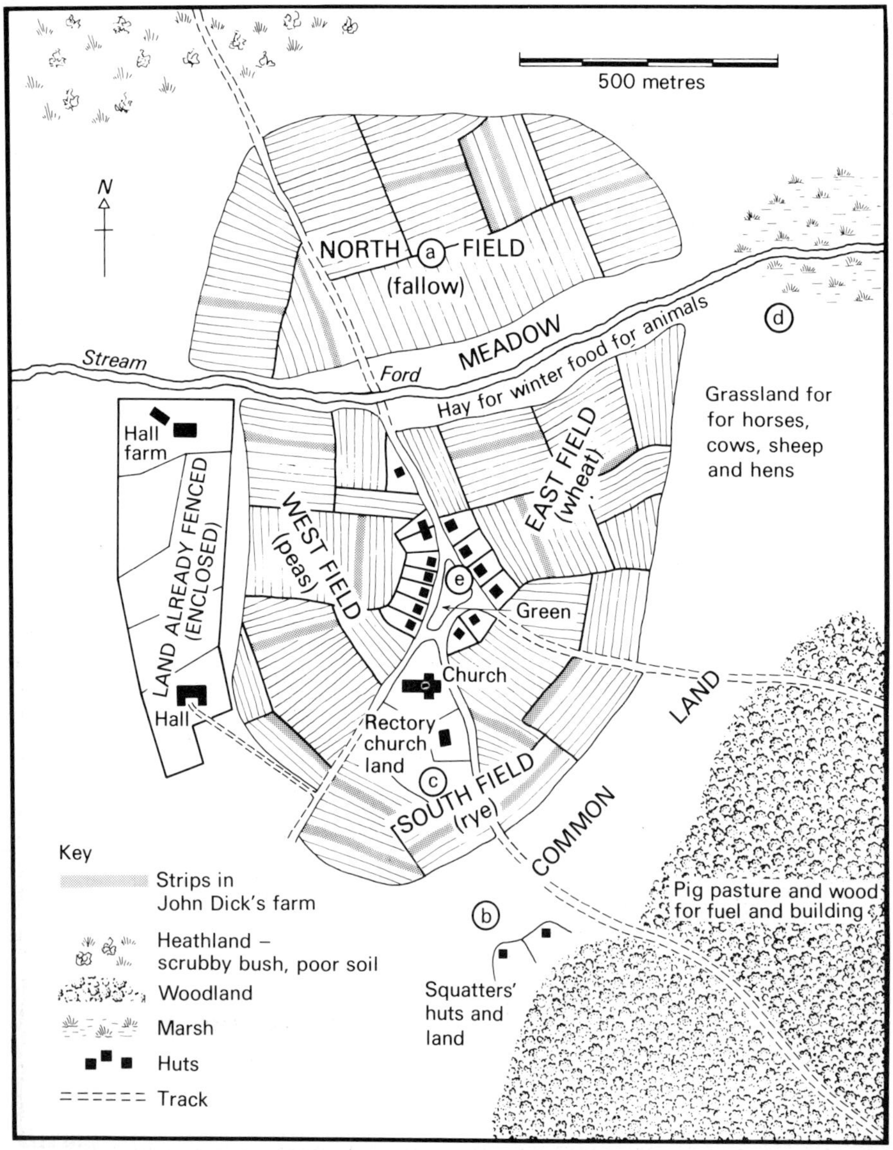

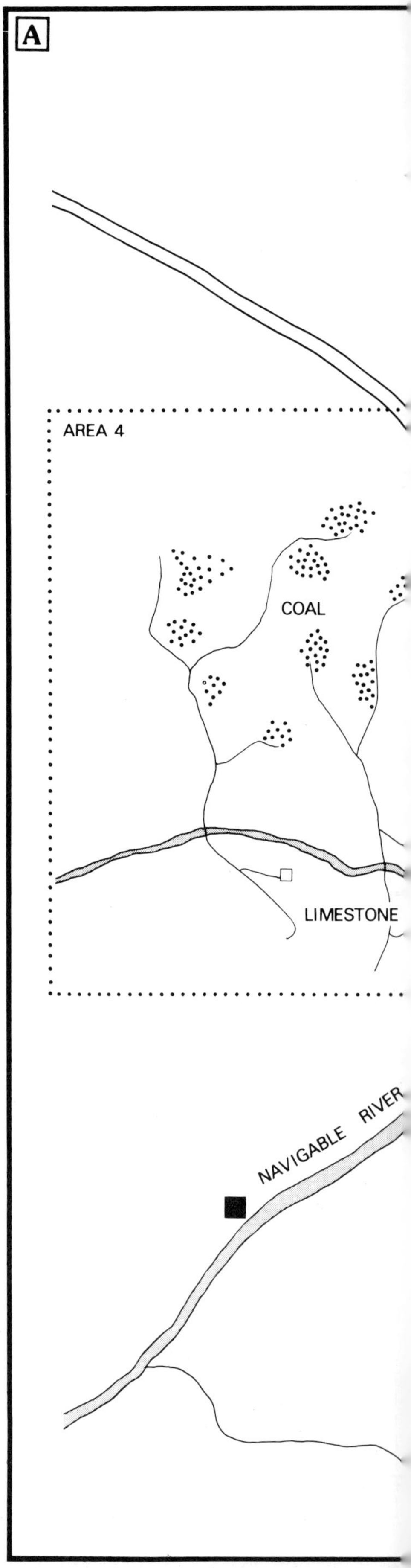

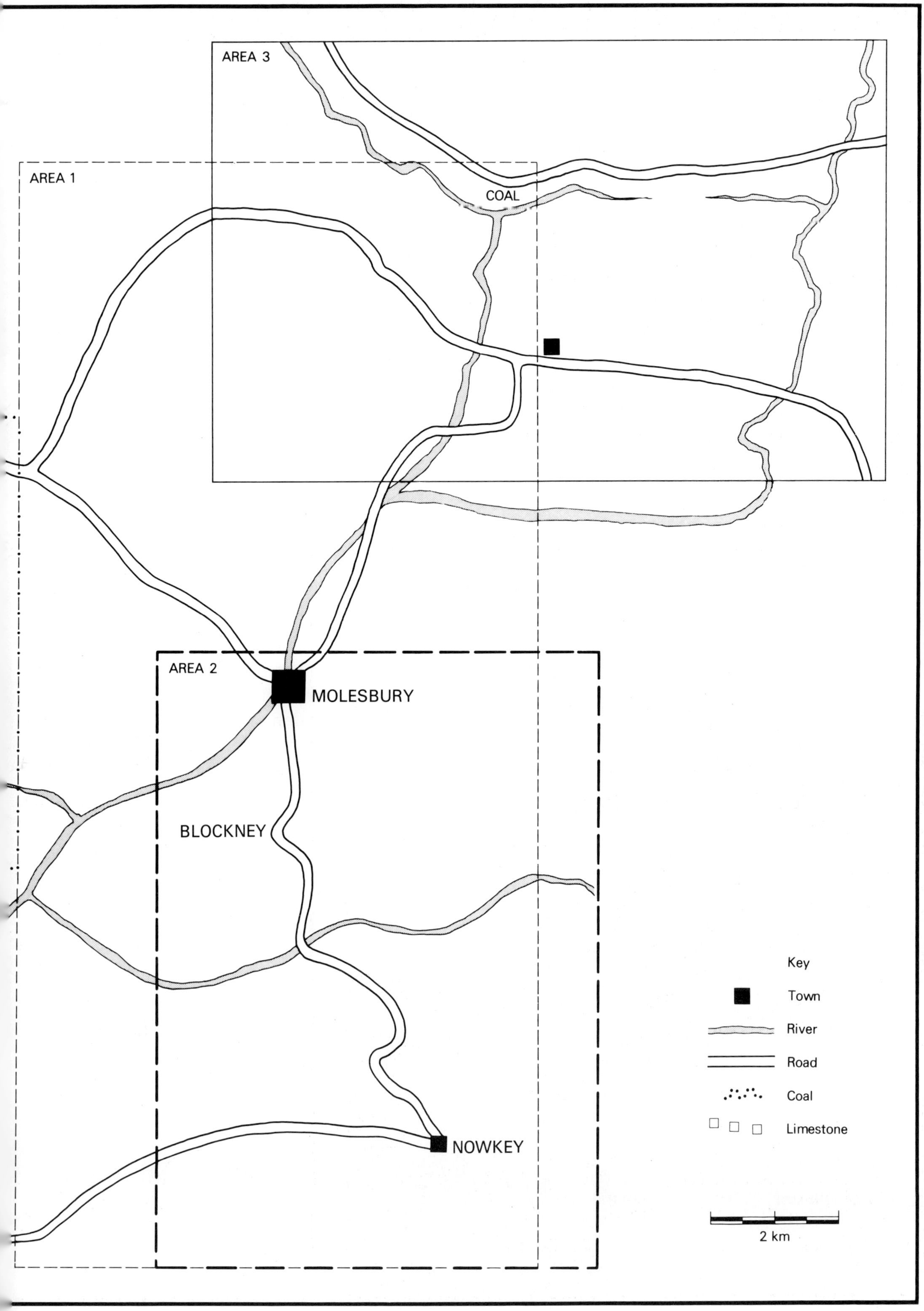
AREA 3
AREA 1
COAL
AREA 2
MOLESBURY
BLOCKNEY
NOWKEY
Key
Town
River
Road
Coal
Limestone
2 km

A

THE AGRICULTURAL REVOLUTION

Before 1740, farmers ran their farms in the old medieval ways. There had only been a few changes—see *The Tudors*, pages 48-51. After 1740 the Agricultural Revolution changed Area **B** on page 6 in many ways. In 1813 a government report said that the new ways of farming had transformed the face of the country. There were five main new ways in which farmers like Fred Dick, John Dick's grandson, ran his farm:

a Farmers grew *new* kinds of crops—e.g. clover and turnips.
b They reared *improved* breeds of animals, like those shown in **A,** and *better* varieties of crops.
c They grew their crops and raised their animals in *new ways*. They no longer left fields *fallow* (see *The Normans*, pages 33, 36). Through the winter they fed turnips and hay to their animals. Before, they used to kill most of them at the beginning of winter, as they did not have enough grain to keep them alive from autumn to spring.
d Farmers *changed* the way they ran their lands. They fenced in or enclosed the common fields and common grazing and woodland, and grouped together land which before had been split up among many strips—see **B** on page 6.
e Farmers began to use *new kinds* of machinery and ploughs—see **B.**

B

Even more important than new methods of farming was a *change of attitude* in how the farmer went about his work. He now farmed to *make money* from the sale of crops. Before, most farmers had only grown enough for their own needs. **C** shows the main farming pioneers and inventions. Why did these changes happen? **D** gives a clue.

C	**New Method or Invention**	**Result**
Jethro Tull *1720s and 30s*	Improved seed drill for sowing seed. Spread ideas about hoeing between rows to kill weeds and make soil fertile.	1733, book *The Horse Hoeing Husbandry* spread ideas already quite common. Very few seed drills used until after 1800.
Viscount Townshend 1730s and 40s	Major Norfolk landowner who used the very common 'Norfolk' rotation—wheat/turnips/barley/clover on his estates. Mixing clay with sandy soil on his large estate helped make it fertile and rich.	Not an innovator. He helped *spread ideas* about the new farming, for he was one of the most powerful and well known men in the country. He is typical of the country's great landowners who used new farming methods to make more money from their estates.
Thomas Coke 1770s and 80s	Changed ways in which he let his land to his tenants. Introduced new breeds of sheep and cattle in Norfolk. Used irrigation on dry soil, improved drains on farms, used new manures. Held 'agricultural shows'.	By 1770s all the new farming methods were already in use on his estate. He too *spread ideas* to smaller farmers.
Robert Bakewell 1745-80	Specialist breeder of farm animals so they would grow bigger more quickly. Bred a new kind of sheep—the Leicester—helped develop the Shire Horse.	One of many animal breeders—his ideas were widely copied. None of his breeds survived in their original form.
Rotherham plough 1730s	New type of plough.	Could now plough with two horses instead of six oxen. Not in common use until after 1800.
McCormick reaper 1850s	Machine for reaping grain.	Became widely used in 1850s—could cut grain much faster.
Threshing machine 1786	Machine for threshing—replaced the use of the hand flail.	Widely used by the 1820s.

D

Increased demand →	**Led to farming changes** →	**Results of changes**
More people to be fed in the growing industrial towns. Raw materials needed for industry.	Better crops and animals. Development of new crops and breeds. New ways of farming and machinery introduced.	Enclosure of common grazing land and common open fields. Change in villages—farmers went to live in new farmhouses on their compact farms.

??????????????????????????

1 What *evidence* do the following give you about changes in farming from 1740:
- **A** (*clue*—sheep, fence)?
- **B** (*clue*—reaping)?

2 Imagine a visit to the village shown in **B** on page 6 in 1740 with John Dick, and again in 1880 (**C** on page 12) with his great-grandson, James Dick. What might you see at the following points: **a, b, c, d, e**?
Make out a table like the one below, with your ideas.

Place on maps	**Seen in 1740**	**Seen in 1880**
a		
b		
c		
d		
e		

3 What was the Agricultural Revolution?

THE CHANGING FARM, 1740-1819

A

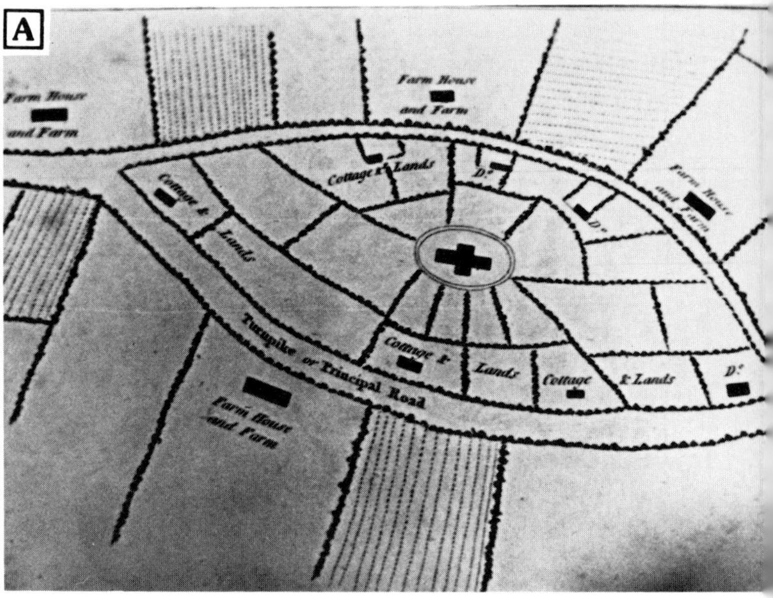

What did the Agricultural Revolution mean for the farmers of Britain? Where fields were grouped together, farmers built new farmhouses and buildings on their new farms. **A** is from an 1813 government report which suggests how a village might be rebuilt after enclosure. The report said that the new farmhouse and buildings for a farm should be:

B

1 *In a central part of the farm.*

2 *A proper distance from the road.*

3 *Have a high, but not exposed aspect* (outlook, view), *so that*

—the farm yard may be warm for young cattle.

—the manure may be carried down hill.

—the liquid manure may be run over as much land as possible.

C is a plan of the buildings of such a farm. **D** is a photograph of a typical new farm.

C

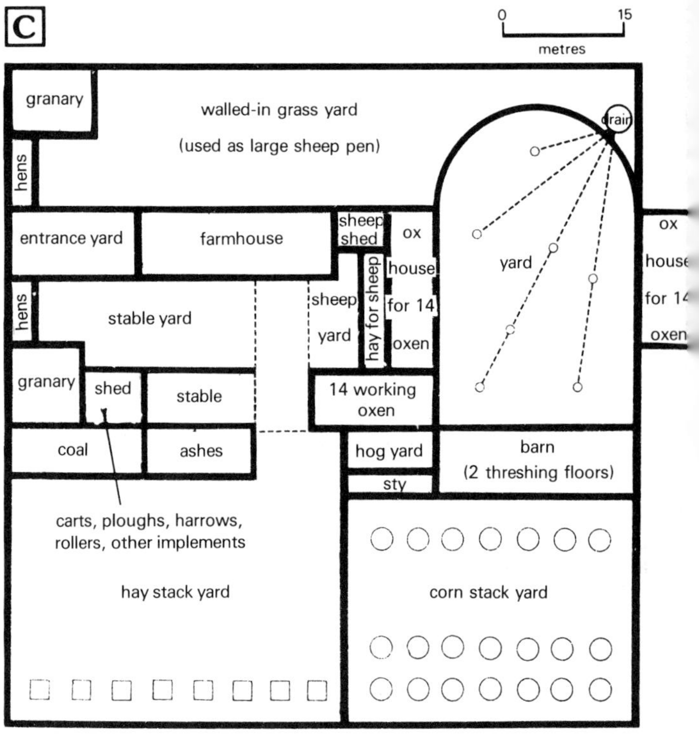

The hedges, roads and fields of new farms were planned to make farming easy. Hedges and roads were usually straight. Fields were laid out so as to be quick to reach from the farmhouse, and to make machinery easy to use on them. The 1813 government report said how the farmer of Hall Farm (see **B** page 6) used a four-year crop rotation, **E**.

D

E

Year	Crop	Notes
1	Wheat 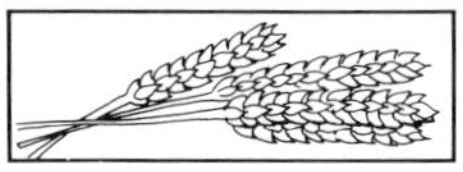	Takes goodness out of soil.
2	Turnips  Sheep 	Feeds animals in winter, allows farmer to clear land of weeds (by hoeing between rows) and enriches soil. Sheep eat turnips and manure soil.
3	Barley 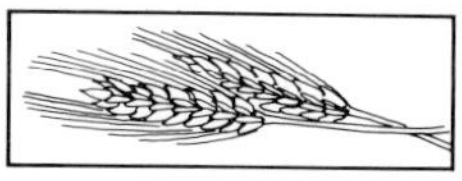	Needs rich soil.
4	Clover  Cows  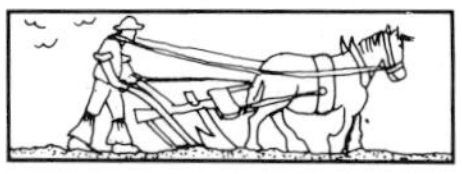	Enriches soil again, and provides winter food for animals. Grazing animals fertilize land with dung. After ploughing, plant wheat for repeat of Year 1.

????????????

1 What reasons do you think there were for a farm in 1800 to:

- **a** have its buildings in the middle of the farm?
- **b** be on high ground?
- **c** be planned like **C**?
- **d** have straight hedges?
- **e** have a four crop rotation like **E**?

2 Imagine you were talking to the farmer of Hall Farm, in the first year of beginning a four-year crop rotation **E**. **F** is the farmer's evidence to the government committee. Say what he might tell you about the farm as he takes you around the fields and buildings. Mention why the farm has been planned out in that way, what crops are grown and why, and what he intends to grow in the next three years. Discuss the new ways of farming. Why are they better than the old?

F **Farmer's evidence 1813**

Divide the ploughed land into four parts, that is for wheat, turnips, barley and clover.

Year One (after the wheat harvest.)
September – October The wheat stubble is harrowed by drawing the harrows one way, which roots up the stubble, and returning back along the same way, drawing up the greatest part of the stubble, which is gathered by the harrows. A person following them with a fork, unloads them, and lays it upon heaps.
November – December The stubble ground is ploughed.

Year Two *March-April* The stubble ground is cross ploughed, and when dry, harrowed. If the weather proves suitable, much of the crouch grass is got out and burned.
May-July In which months the fallows have three ploughings and sufficient harrowings to prepare for turnips. For which I laid out about eight cubic yards of reduced dung, or 72 bushels of clod lime upon each acre, which was ploughed in at the last ploughing. *7th June – 14th July*. Turnip seed, one pound to the acre, sowed, the plants twice hoed.
November The turnip crop . . . draw home those under the hedges, and some of the largest over the rest of the field. When the tops and roots are cut off, carry them home, and place them in heaps of about 12 cart loads each, in the form of the cone of a wheat rick. Cover a foot thick with straw and thatch. These serve as a resource in time of frost and snow for the beasts that are stall fed, of which I generally have 20 yearly. A man and boy, with one horse and cart, supplies them, leaving as many turnips to be eaten upon the land with sheep, as to ensure fertility enough for the crops of barley . . . . Another advantage obtained by stall feeding with turnips is making a large quantity of straw into manure. (Sheep are kept through the winter in the turnip fields in a fenced area. Straw is used for bedding.)

Year Three *March-April* As the land becomes cleared of its crop of turnips, it is ploughed and harrowed . . . end of April was sowed with 3½ statute bushels of barley, 14lbs of common red clover seed and one peck of fine rye grass seed to each acre. The average crop about 50 statute bushels of barley (each acre).

Year Four *May* The young clover not eaten between December and May, the part mowed, on an average produces about two wagon loads of hay or a ton (each acre).
October Plough in nine inch furrows and six inches deep, and sow with 2 bushels of wheat, produces about seventeen bushels of wheat (each acre).

Year One The winter wheat is harvested. Start of rotation again.

ENCLOSURE

The fencing in—*enclosure*—of open fields like those on page 4 was common after 1700 – **A.** **B** shows the main farming areas in 1740. From 1740 to 1801 enclosure could happen by private agreement between landowners, or by an Act of Parliament for a particular village. Parliament agreed to enclosure if the owners of most of the land wanted it. After a General Enclosure Act of 1801 a village could enclose if the owners of four-fifths of the land asked for it. **C** shows the share-out of the lands of Blockney after an Enclosure Act in 1813. The Act appointed commissioners to parcel out the land among the different landowners. Their *enclosure award* laid down the farm boundaries.

A Number of enclosure bills each year, 1760-1830

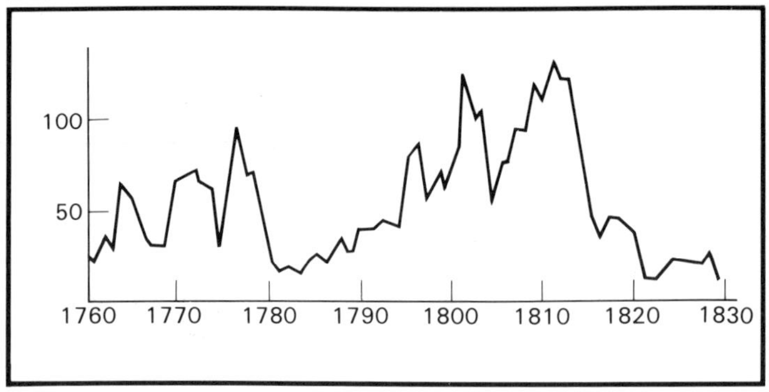

B

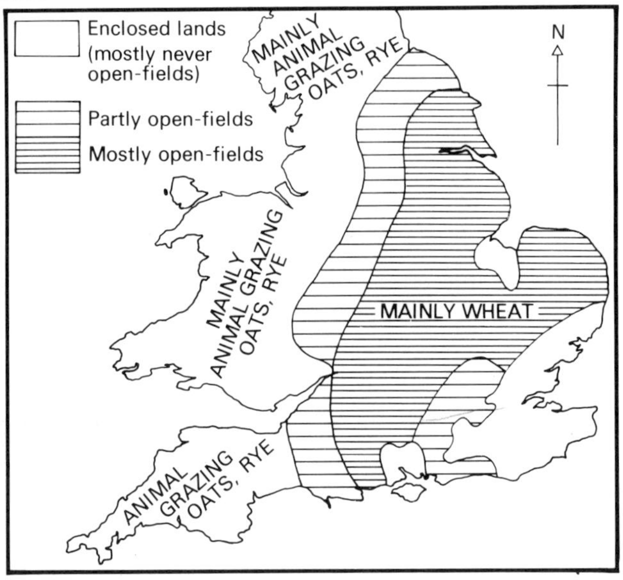

C

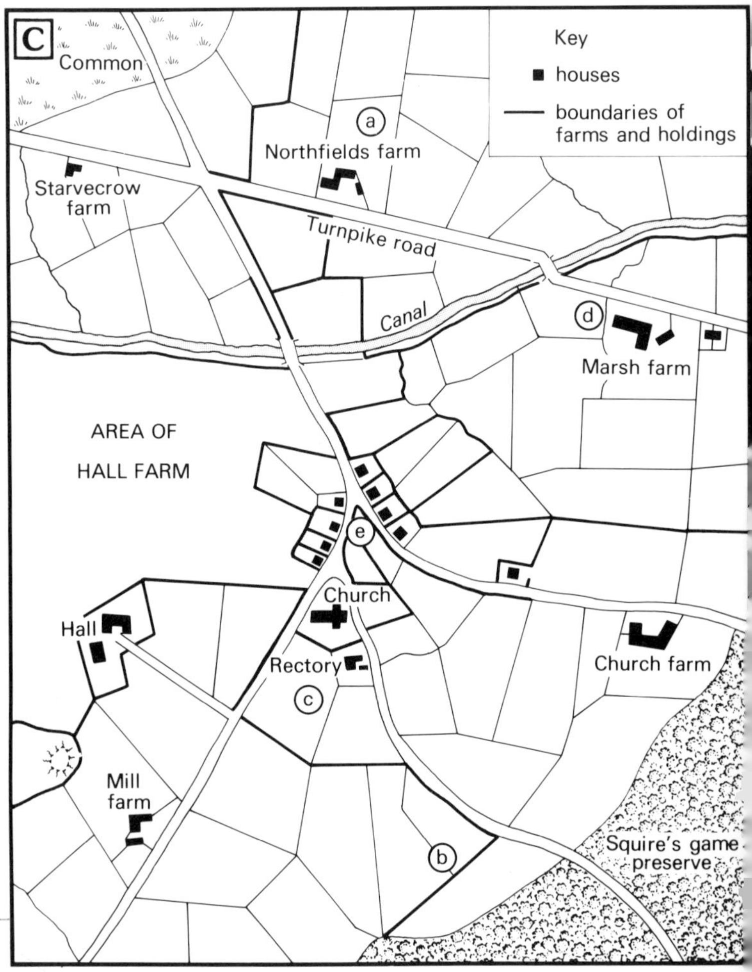

D **Points for and against enclosure**

1 Enclosure meant that the land could be farmed more efficiently. The land in new farms was put in a block. The farmer could get to his land much more easily. Before, he had to travel around between his strips. Animals could be better looked after than on the common land. The farmer could plan for himself how he farmed his own land, instead of having to do only what the rest of the villagers agreed to do. Now he could have a much better balance between the different kinds of crops, and between crops and grassland.

2 Lands could be more profitably farmed. Often unenclosed common and open field land was worn out. It needed to be ploughed up, manured, drained and reseeded. New crops could now be grown.

3 New farms were larger than before, because they included the owner's share of the common.

4 Enclosure often meant an end to paying tithes (taxes to the church).

5 Small freeholders and copyholders and even squatters would get their rights to land confirmed. The commissioners who shared out the land were often very fair. However, sometimes the squatters would lose the land they farmed.

6 Land prices would double, from £15 to £30 an acre.

7 It was easy to borrow money to pay for the costs of enclosure—about 50p an acre in 1813.

8 If a landowner let his land at a fixed rent for a long time ahead, he would have to pay the cost of enclosure but would not be able to get the extra money back from his tenants.

On their enclosed lands farmers tried out many new ideas for the growing of crops and the raising of animals throughout the 19th century. How they farmed depended on what their land was like – for example whether it was hilly or on low lying clay. In 1881 a Royal Commission on Agriculture looked at how farmers cultivated their soil. On 7 December 1881 it heard evidence from Mr J. Prout of Bishop's Stortford, Hertfordshire. On his 450 acre farm he used a rotation of wheat, barley, oats and a few turnips with 50 acres under clover. The Commissioners asked him about his steam ploughing:

E *"What is the difference in cost between ploughing by steam and ploughing by horses?" "It costs at least 50 per cent less to plough by steam . . . we can plough about eight acres a day with a four furrowed plough: and four horses would scarcely plough one acre. Therefore the steam engine is doing the work of 32 horses . . . and the good point is that you can do the work at the right time, and that is very important on heavy land."*

"You can get upon the land with the steam engine when you cannot get upon it with horses: is that what you mean?" "If the land after harvest is very dry, as it sometimes is, that is perhaps the best time; you can scarcely work horses at the time when the land is hard, but you can work the steam plough."

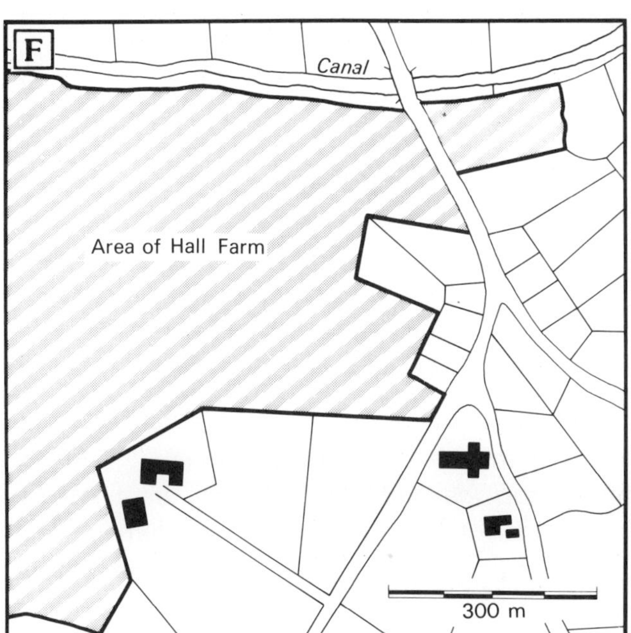

Mr Prout also used manure upon his farm. Most common was *guano*—bird muck—from Peru. This gave him the chemicals his crops—wheat, barley, turnips and oats—needed in order to grow.

1 In what order of importance do you think Fred Dick, John Dick's grandson, (see pages 8 and 9) would place the points in favour of enclosure put forward in 1812?

2 Fred Dick had to reorganize his land—see **B** on page 6 — after the 1812 Enclosure Award. **F** is his new 160 acre farm. What would you advise him to do? Use the evidence above, and on pages 8-11, to do the following:

a Choose a site for the farmhouse.
b Plan out the farmhouse and buildings, like **C** on page 10. Label what each is used for.
c Say what machinery the farm would need.
d Draw in the boundaries of the fields. Each field should be ten acres in size. Name the fields.
e Say what crops you would grow in the fields in the first year of a four-year crop rotation.
f Plan the crops for the next year.
g Put in tracks and roads.

3 You are a farmer in 1880. Write a letter to a friend pointing out the advantages of ploughing with steam over ploughing with horses.

4 Look carefully at the enclosed Hall Farm, and the village of Blockney. How do you think enclosure changed the way the countryside looked? Say how the following might have changed between 1800 and 1880:

a the hedging and ditching of the land;
b the buildings in the village, and its lands;
c how the land was farmed, and what was grown in the fields;
d the common land;
e roads and tracks.

THE CHANGING VILLAGE

The village of Wortham, Suffolk. The local vicar, Richard Cobbold, kept a note and sketch book. In it he made a record of the people, their lives and their homes from 1830 onwards. How had the changes in farming affected them? Many local gentlemen lived in new houses, built in the last hundred years. Henry Balding:

A *. . . has built the mansion called The Grove, and has most elegantly furnished it.*

There were a number of well-off farmers, **B**. Mr William Read was one.

C *The farm belongs to Miss Harrison and is run by Mr Wm Read and was so by his father before him. Both of them are Townwardens or Churchwardens for the Parish of Wortham. One of the features of Wortham . . . was the late tenant who was to be seen daily with his long whip and good old chestnut horse rising through the fields of his farm or on the roads of his parish. He very seldom went from home . . . . A good farmer, a good employer, a kind-hearted upright man.*

Ted and Rose Collins worked for William Read. Cobbold tells us that Ted was:

D *. . . one of the best men who ever lived in his class of life, I may almost say in any, if honesty and integrity, steadiness and faithfulness, activity and energy be qualities to be admired. Was the best labourer in the parish. Up early, constant to his work, and understood all branches of farming from the hedgerow to the plough—and from pigs and poultry to cows and horses. More, he was always to be depended on. . . . Rose Collins, his wife still lives with him in the Cottage near Mr and Mrs Read. She was once a very active farming woman, understood poultry* (hens, geese etc.), *a most capital dairy woman and in every respect an honest woman.*

B

E was a typical village scene in the pub. In the village were many poor people. They spent much time in the local inn. Ned Flatman was typical:

F *Now Ned Flatman was a drunkard to the day of his death! Never attended any place of public worship and never attended a Church till he was carried into it.*

When they grew too old to work, or there was none for them, the village poor hated the idea of going to live in the *workhouse*. In the nineteenth century there were no old age pensions. Thomas Goddard was typical:

G *He was so punctual to his work as a labourer that his master never knew him a minute too late any one morning he went to work and not a minute too early when he left off. Nobody could ever compel this man to go into a workhouse. He never deserved a prison, he used to say, and he never would go into one!*

E

. . . He died in a miserable hovel—in fact an outhouse.

H is a list of jobs in a Yorkshire village from 1750-1800.

H

56 labourers	2 clockmakers
7 yeomen	1 weaver
27 farmers	1 beggar
7 gardeners	10 tailors
4 servants	1 surgeon
1 gamekeeper	2 joiners
9 gentlemen	1 saddler
5 paupers	1 baker
6 masons	1 parish clerk
5 butchers	1 schoolmistress
4 carpenters	1 thatcher
3 blacksmiths	2 pinmakers
1 wheelwright	1 milliner
1 woodcutter	1 cook
11 colliers	1 cooper
2 millers	1 innkeeper
2 basketmakers	1 excise officer
1 chandler	1 turnpike keeper

? ? ? ? ? ? ? ? ? ? ? ?

1 What ideas do you get of the following people from the *evidence* about them?

Henry Balding—**A**
William Read—**B, C**
Ted Collins—**D**
Rose Collins—**D**
Ned Flatman—**F**
Thomas Goddard—**G**

2 What kind of farming do you think was carried on by William Read?

3 Use the *evidence* on these pages to write a story about the village in the form of an interview in 1870 between yourself and the vicar Richard Cobbold.
Ask him how the village, and the lives of the villagers, might have changed in the past hundred years. To help you, look at changes in farming (pages 10-13), the coming of the turnpike (pages 16-17, picture **F**) and the railway (pages 28-31).

THE TRANSPORT REVOLUTION: ROADS

How easy was it to get along the roads to school this morning? Compare the road outside your house to the ones in **A** and **B.** Do you think you would be able to drive a car along the road shown in **A**? Two hundred years ago a writer said about a road like the one from his house to the nearest school:

C *It is for near twelve miles so narrow that a mouse cannot pass by any carriage. I saw a fellow creep under his wagon to help me if possible to lift my chaise over a hedge. The ruts are of an incredible depth. The trees everywhere overgrow the road, so that it is totally hidden from the sun, except at a few places . . . I must not forget always meeting with chalk wagons, themselves frequently stuck fast.*

In 1706 local merchants and traders told the MP for Droitwich that the roads between Droitwich and Worcester were:

D *. . . so very much destroyed by the great carriage of salt, iron, coal and other wares, that they are almost impassable, several carts and wagons having been there broke, the goods spoiled and many horses lost, and the inhabitants are unable to repair them.*

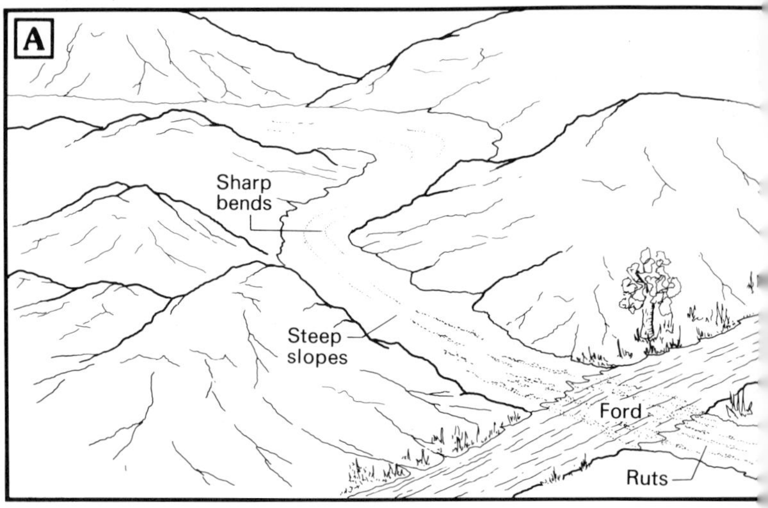

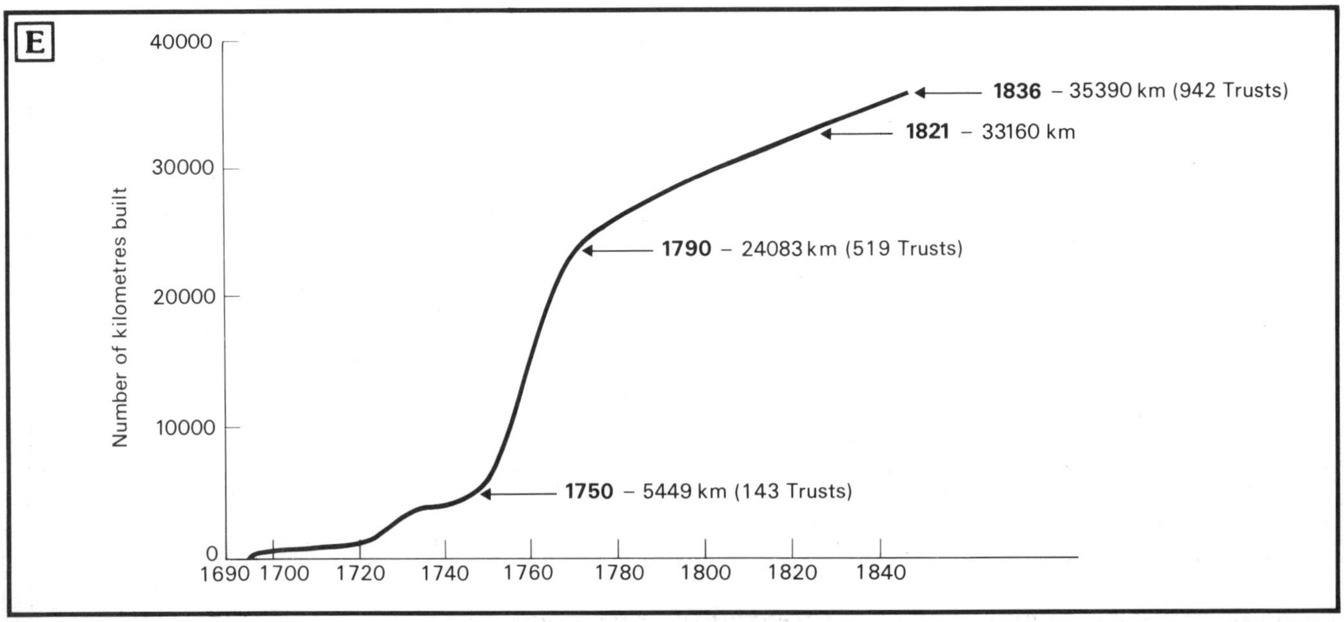

F **The turnpike road network in the south of England in 1720 and 1750**

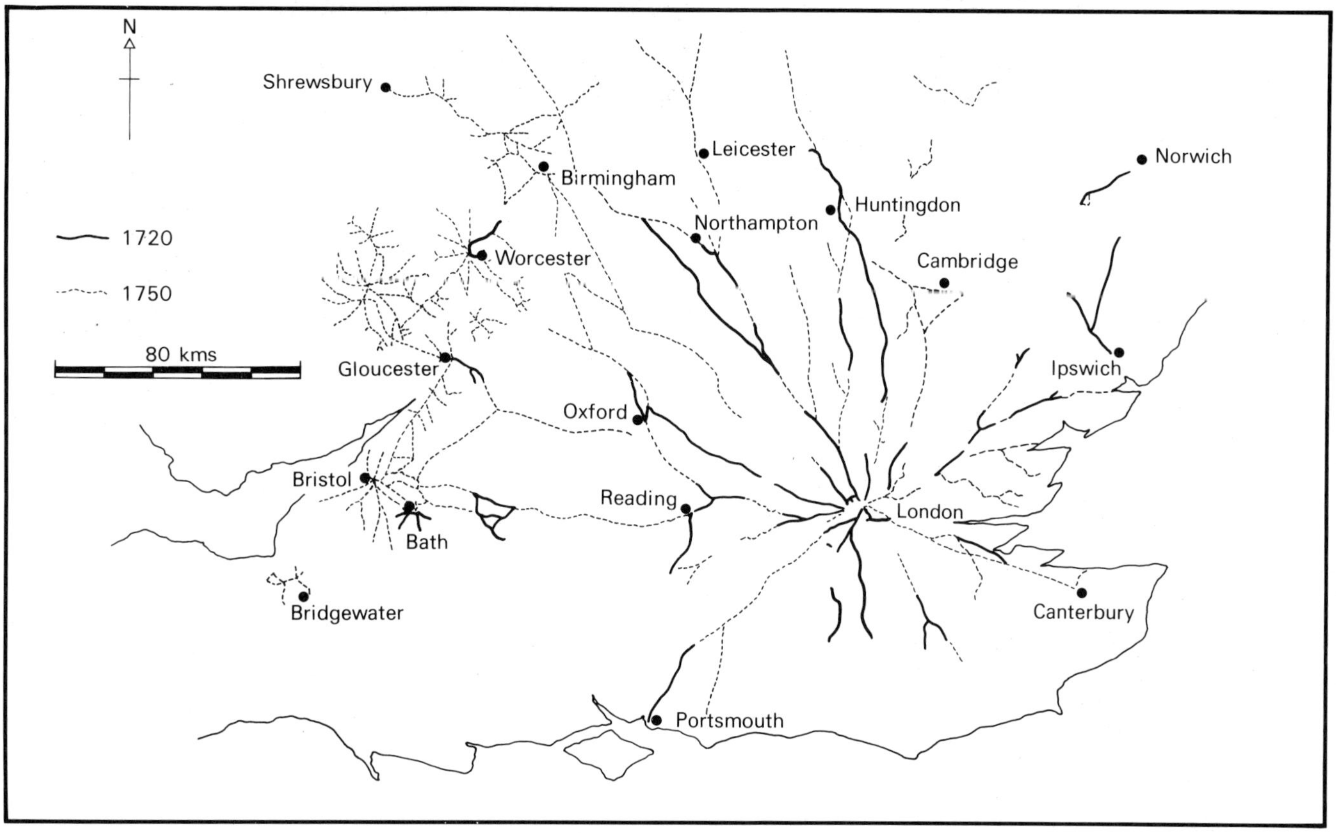

The people of Droitwich had an answer to the problem of their road to Worcester. They asked or *petitioned* Parliament to let them build a new road, a *turnpike* road—between the two towns. They hoped Parliament would allow local landowners, merchants and traders to buy shares in a new firm or company—a *turnpike trust*. The trust would use the money from its shares to build the road. It would then look after it. To pass along the road travellers would have to pay cash—*tolls*. This money would be used to mend the road.

The first turnpike road was built in 1663. It was only in the 1690s that they became popular as the best way to improve the country's roads. Between 1720 and 1770 they spread very quickly—**E. F** shows the growing network in the South of England.

??????????????????????????

1 Quiz Time Answer the following questions:
a What problems would face you if you tried to drive a car along road **A**?
b What happened to the chalk wagons?
c Why was the road ruined between Droitwich and Worcester?
d What was a turnpike road?
e What was a turnpike trust?
f What was a toll?
g When did turnpikes become popular?

2 Draw a map of the South of England in 1750, and show on it the turnpike roads to London from: Portsmouth, Canterbury, Ipswich, Leicester, Cambridge, Worcester, Bristol.

3 Imagine you were going from Leicester to Bath in 1750. Plan your four-day turnpike journey, saying where you will stay.

4 Why did the Droitwich traders want a turnpike road to be built?

5 What effect do you think the turnpikes had on life in these towns?

ROADS: 2

Turnpikes meant that people could travel much more easily and quickly. **A** and **B** give an idea of how travel speeded up.

The fastest way to travel was by stagecoach. In 1784 the first Royal Mail coach ran from Bath to London. By 1820 coaches ran between all the main towns—**C. D** is a typical coaching scene.

There were several ways to build turnpike roads. Three of the most famous road builders were John Metcalfe (1717-80) from Yorkshire, John MacAdam (1756-1836), and Thomas Telford (1757-1834).

Telford's most famous road was **E**—from London to Holyhead. Between 1815 and 1830 he built a new road. He had to put up over 1000 new bridges, including the Menai Suspension Bridge linking Anglesey to Wales. Telford built many other roads, including over 1000 miles in Scotland. He also put up buildings, and dug docks and canals, see pages 24-25.

By 1840 the turnpike age was over. The railway was a new and rapidly growing form of travel. Local government began to take over the running of roads from the turnpike trusts. **F** shows the steps involved.

A **The improvement in the time taken to travel from London to other cities**

London	1750	1770
Bristol	3 days	2 days
Shrewsbury	4 days	2 days
Liverpool	3 days	2 days
Edinburgh	12 days	4 days
Newcastle	6 days	3 days
York	4 days	2 days

B **Time allowed for the running of the Edinburgh to London stagecoach**

General Poſt-Office.

The Earl of CHESTERFIELD, AND The Earl of LEICESTER, Poſtmaſter-General

Edinburgh to London Time-Bill.

	Miles	Time allowed H.	M	
				Diſpatched from the Poſt-Office, Edinburgh, the of 179 at 3.45 Coach Nº ſent out With a Time-Piece ſafe Nº to
Dryſdale	18½	2	30	Arrived at Haddington at 6.15
Clark	11	1	30	Arrived at Dunbar at 7 45
Lorimer	15	2	10	Arrived at Preſs at 9.55
Hume	11½	1	50	Arrived at Lerwick at 11.45 Delivered the Time-piece ſafe to Coach Nº gone forward
			30	*To be at Berwick by Forty-five Minutes paſt Eleven, where Half an Hour is allowed for Supper*
Dixon	15½	2	10	Arrived at Belford at 2.25
M'Donnel	14½	2	0	Arrived at Alnwick at 4.25
Wilſon	9½	1	20	Arrived at Felton at 5.45
Nelſon	10	1	20	Arrived at Morpeth at 7.5
Hall	15	2	0	Arrived at Newcaſtle at 9.5 Delivered the Time-Piece ſafe to Coach Nº gone forward
		×	30	*Thirty Minutes allowed for Breakfaſt, &c To leave Newcaſtle at 10 o'Clock*
	14½	2	0	Arrived at Durham at 12.—
			15	*Fifteen Minutes allowed for Office Buſineſs*
Wrangham	9	1	15	Arrived at Ruſhyford at 1.30
Trenham	9	1	10	Arrived at Darlington at 2.45
			15	*Fifteen Minutes allowed for Office Buſineſs*
Smith	16	2	5	Arrived at Northallerton at 5–5 Delivered the Time-Piece ſafe to

C **Mail coach routes in 1820**

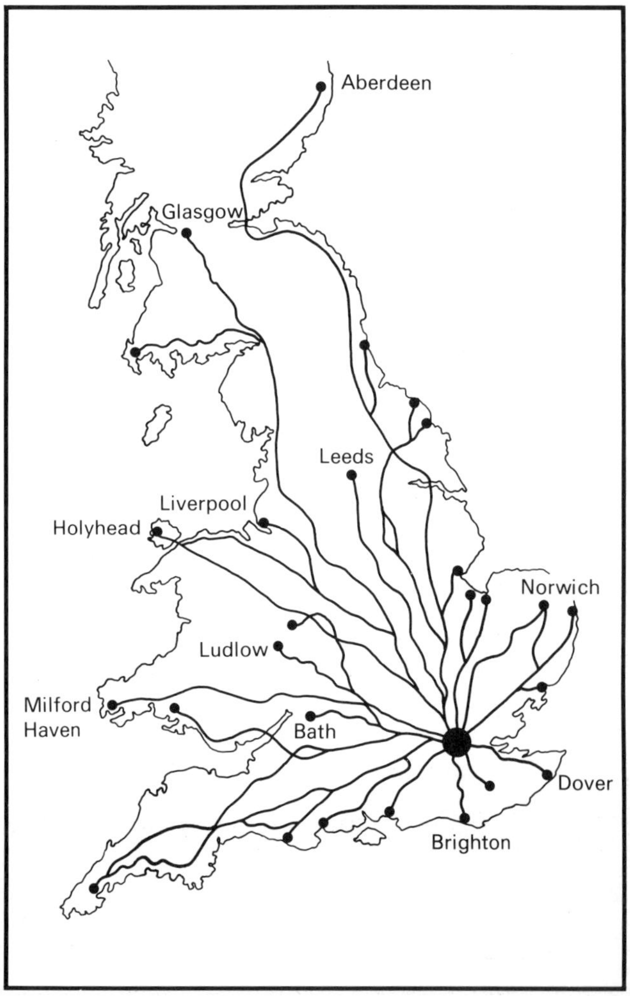

D

E

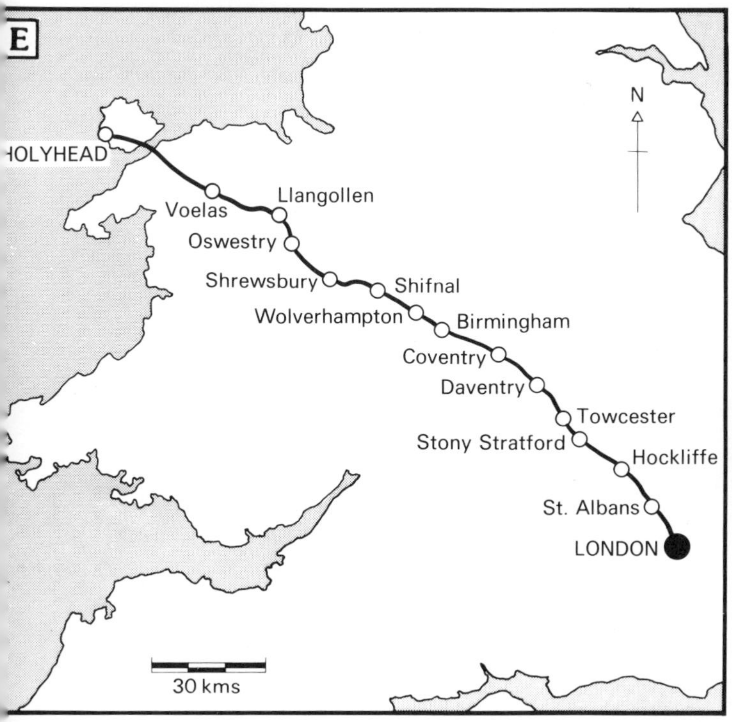

F

Year	Change
1862	*General Highways Act* Highway districts, each made up of several parishes, set up to maintain roads.
1864	*Parliamentary Committee enquiry into turnpikes* Report condemned the turnpike system. Parliament began to refuse to allow turnpike trusts to continue their work. Quick fall in number of trusts.
1881	Total of turnpike trusts down to 184.
1883	Turnpike trusts abolished in Scotland.
1888	*Local Government Act.* Running of main roads handed over to new county councils. Care of minor roads given to district councils.
1890	Turnpike trusts down to two.
1895	Turnpike trusts abolished.

1 Transport Quiz

a How long did it take a coach to travel from Newcastle to London in 1750 and in 1770?

b Why had coach travel speeded up?

c Who was Telford?

d When did county councils take over main roads?

e Why were turnpike trusts found to be a poor way to run the roads in 1864?

2 What does **D** tell you about travel in the turnpike age? Mention what you can see at **a, b, c, d.**

3 Use a large scale map to trace Telford's Holyhead—London road. What problems do you think he faced in building it?

4 Use the evidence on this page, and pages 16-17, 20-21, and anything else you can find out, to write your own history of the turnpike age.

ROADS: HISTORY AROUND US

A

B

C

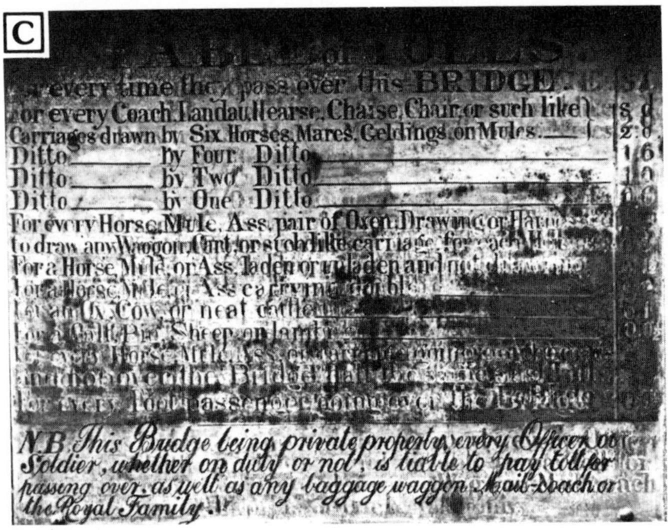

Near where you live, and on your way to school, you will find some remains of turnpike roads. What evidence of turnpikes can you still see? In the town or village there might be a turnpike coaching inn like the one in **D** on page 19. By the roadside you will find milestones made from metal, brick or stone, **A.** Travellers paid their tolls at toll houses like **B.** Many still survive. The toll gate will very likely have gone, as well as the toll board, **C.** It told you what you would have to pay for using the road. Often a completely new road will have been built, like **D.**

D

? ? ? ? ? ? ? ? ? ? ? ?

1 Find and record as many of the turnpike features on this page as you can find in your area.

2 Imagine you were with one of the spacemen (pages 4-5) when they visited a local tollhouse keeper in 1840, just after the building of his turnpike. What might he tell you about the changes in road travel in the previous fifty years?

Mention:

Building of turnpikes; kinds of road surfaces; new routes; mail coaches; changes in carts and carriages; a day in his life.

Use **C** to help you.

TRANSPORT REVOLUTION - TURNPIKE!

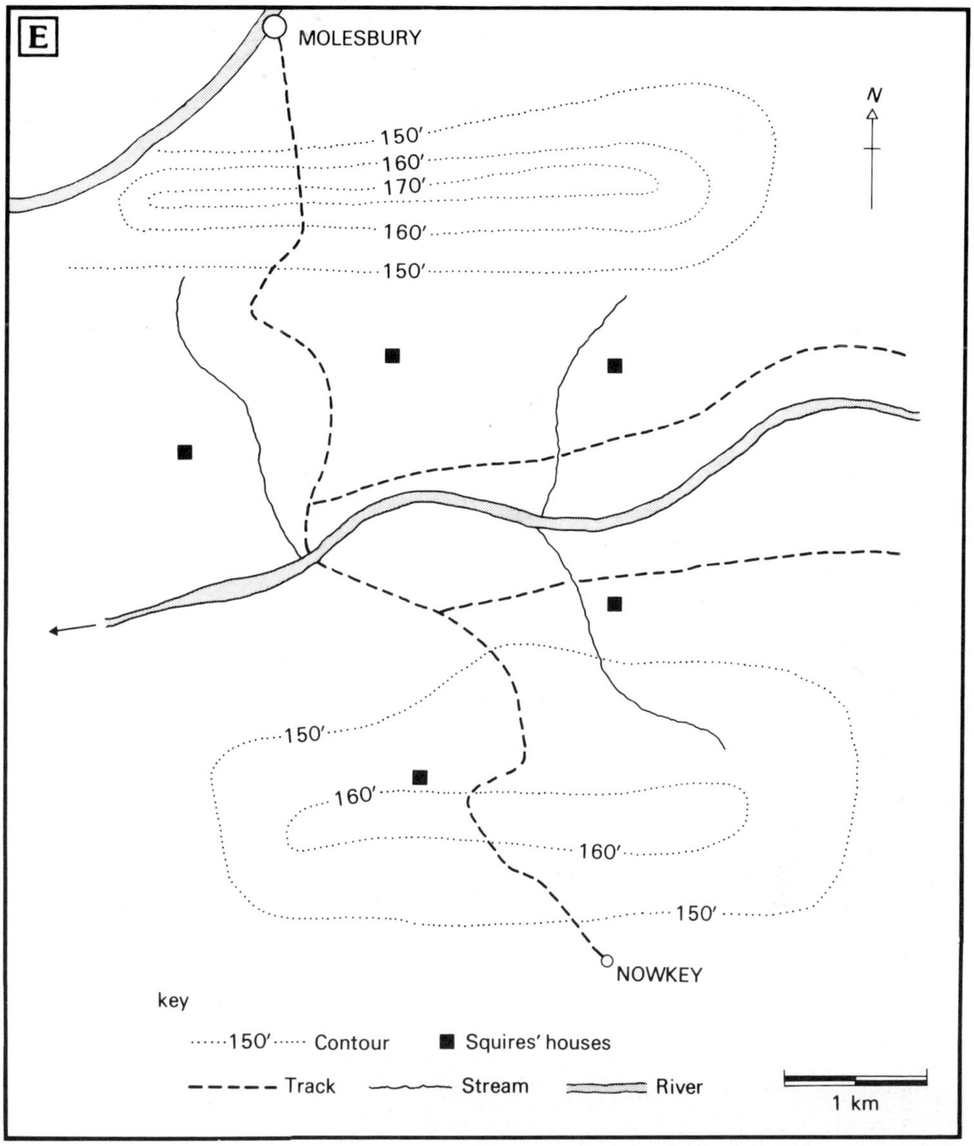

Draw in your features like this:

bridge

turnpike road

tollhouse **T**

milestone

inn **P**

Map **E** shows an area which has a track running through it. The track is the main road between two towns, **Molesbury** and **Nowkey**, page 7. Several local tradesmen, farmers and squires have decided to make the track better. In winter it becomes a sea of mud, and its potholes fill with water. Last year a man walking along the road fell in a pothole and drowned.

Last year, 1770, the MPs for Molesbury and Nowkey got a Turnpike Act through Parliament. The Act sets up a turnpike company to build a new road between the two towns. The owners of the company have asked road builders to put forward plans for the road. The company will choose whoever makes the best plans to build the road. The plans will show the best route, and how it will be built. Imagine you are a road builder. Hand in your plan for the route, with a cross section of your road.

Draw a plan of a toll board, with the charge you will make.

Your road should have the following features.

a No sharp bends.

b No steep slopes which will be hard for carts and carriages to climb.

c The road must pass at least half a kilometre from the house of the squires.

d There will be a bridge where it crosses a stream or river (cost £100 each).

e At each end, and where other tracks join it, there will be a tollhouse and turnpike gate (cost £50 each).

f Every mile there will be a milestone (cost £5 each).

g At each end, and half way along, there will be a site for a coaching inn (no cost).

Draw in your features on the map.

Write a report to send in with your plan, saying why you planned your route with those features.

CANALS

Map **A** shows the rivers which trading ships and barges sailed along in the 1740s. Can you think what problems there were? Locks, weirs, cuttings and tow paths meant that barges could carry heavy loads on rivers. It was a short step from improving rivers to building canals. In 1755 the Sankey brook in Lancashire was heavily *canalised.* In 1761 James Brindley, an engineer, built the first canal in England, from the Duke of Bridgewater's colliery at Worsley to Manchester. Such canals meant that it was much cheaper to carry heavy goods like coal by canal than by road. In 1763 the *Gentleman's Magazine* tells us:

B *At Barton Bridge, Brindley has erected a navigable canal in the air, for it is as high as the tops of the trees. Whilst I was looking at it with a mixture of wonder and delight, four barges*

A

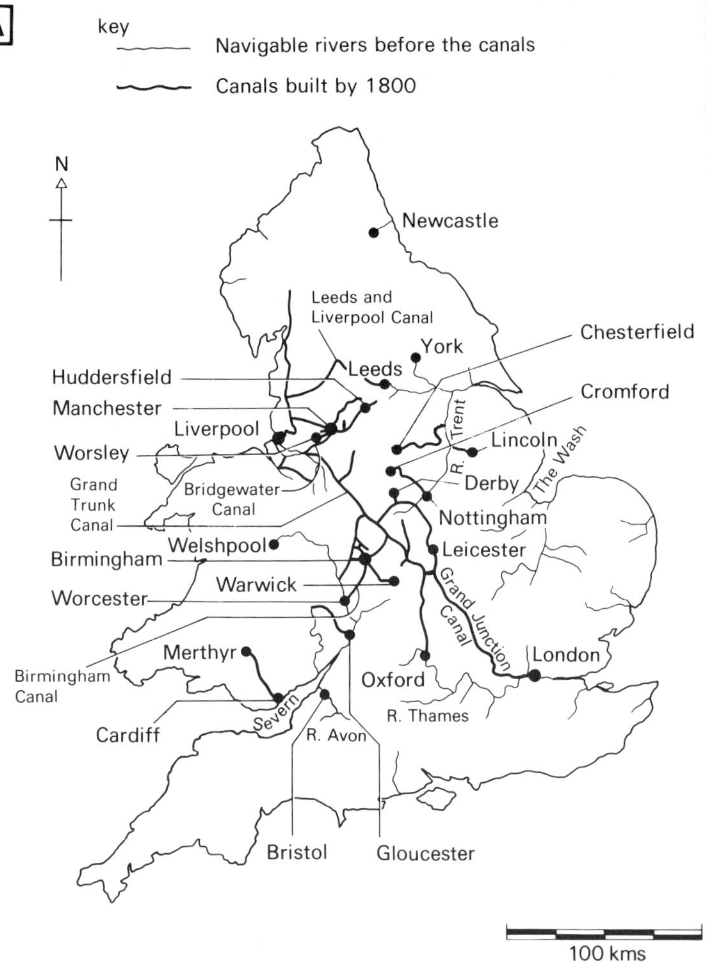

C

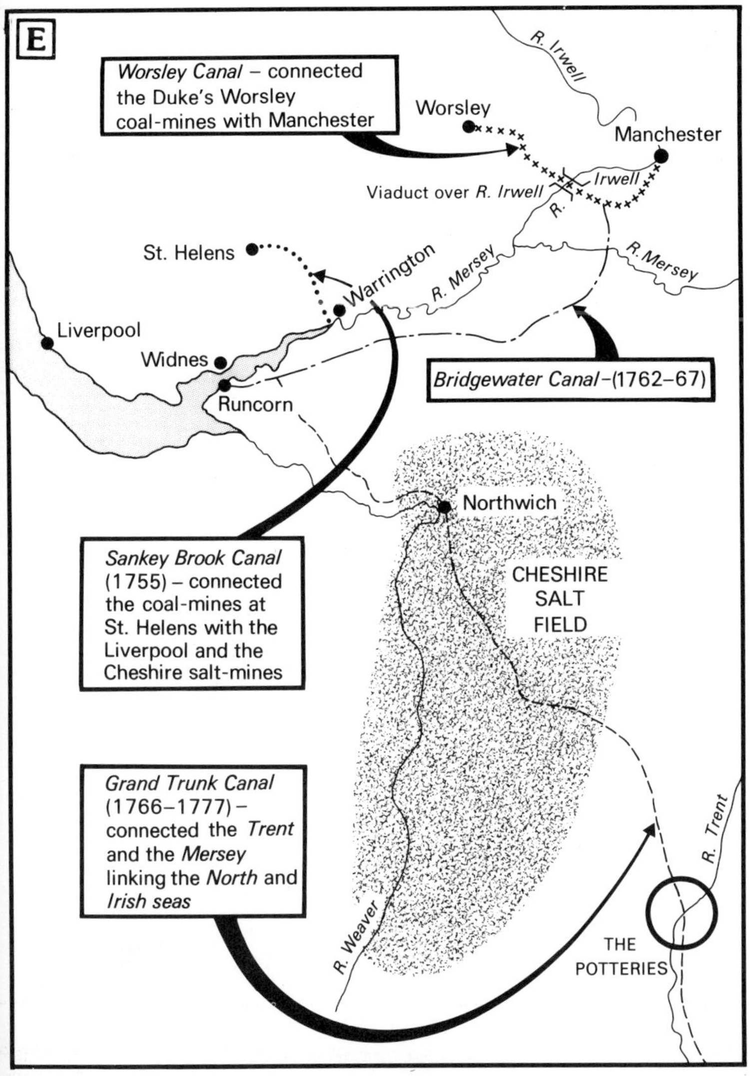

passed me in the space of about three minutes, tow of them being chained together and dragged by two horses, who went on the terras of the canal, whereon, I must own, I dared hardly venture to walk, as I almost trembled to behold the large River Irwell underneath me, across which this navigation is carried by a bridge.

F **Cost of sending a ton of coal from Liverpool to Birmingham in 1790**

C is a picture of the scene described in **B.** The story goes on:

D *The navigation* (canal) *begins at the foot of some hills, in which the Duke's coals are dug, from whence a canal is cut through rocks, which daylight never enters. By this means large boats are hauled to the innermost parts of those hills, and being there filled with coals, are brought out by an easy current, which supplies the whole navigation for the space of about ten miles.*

E gives a clue about why canals were built. The cost of carrying a ton of goods from Liverpool to the Potteries by road was £2 10s (£2.50); by canal it was only 13s 4d (67p). Soon a network of canals linked up the main rivers, cities and towns, **A.** An example was the finishing in 1777 of the Trent – Mersey canal, which joined the two rivers. In the 1790s the boom in canal building was so great that it was called 'canal mania'.

1 **F** gives a clue why canals spread quickly. On map **E**, what kinds of goods do you think canal boats carried from:
Northwich to St Helens
St Helens to Northwich
Liverpool to the Potteries
The Potteries to Liverpool
Worsley to Manchester
Manchester to Liverpool (clue, pages 28-29)

2 Describe **C.** Say what you can see at points **a, b, c, d,** and **e.**

3 Imagine you were planning to send a barrel of oysters from London to a friend in Kendal in 1750. Plan your route, and work out the problems you might have had.

Plan a similar journey in 1790—in what ways would it have changed for the better?

4 What advantages might the canals have had for the following:
Richard Arkwright (see pages 38-39)?
William Reynolds (see pages 48-49)?

CANALS: HISTORY AROUND US

Thomas Telford (see pages 18 – 19) also built canals. **A** shows the ones he built in the Midlands. One such canal was the Shrewsbury Canal. Telford built it in 1795 – 96. The photographs are of what survives today. There may well be canal remains like this near you. Telford wrote that where the canal started:

B *is an inclined plane* (see pages 48 – 49) *of 223 yards in length, and 25 feet of fall. From the bottom of the inclined plane, the canal passes on by Eyton Mill to Long Lane, being a distance of about 4 miles, and in which it rises through locks by 79 feet. From thence it passes on to Long, where it crosses a valley of considerable length, and over the river Tern, at the height of 16 feet above the level of the surface of the meadow, by means of an aqueduct* (see **C**). *Near to this place it crosses the turnpike road, which leads to High Ercall from Wellington . . . it passes on through Withington to near Atcham, where it crosses a turnpike road* (see **D**). *At half a mile to the north of the road it enters a tunnel of 970 yards in length* (see **E**). *. . . it passes along the banks of the river Severn, and ends in a large basin and coal yard. . .*

Telford described the Tern aqueduct:

F *. . . the canal passes over the valley of the Tern at Long, for a distance of 52 yards, upon an aqueduct made all of cast iron. I believe this to be the first aqueduct for the purpose of a navigable canal which has ever been made with this metal.*

Telford explains why the canal was built:

G *The town of Shrewsbury, and the country immediately around it, are supplied with coal principally* (mainly) *from the neighbourhood of Oakengates. Previously it had been carried by land carriage* (carts) *about fourteen miles along the London road. This part of the road, from the constant succession* (passage) *of heavy coal carriages, had become almost impassable, notwithstanding* (despite) *the large sums of money which were annually* (each year) *laid out* (spent) *upon the repairs of it. The price of coals at Shrewsbury continued to rise year after year, and there was no hope of being able to put a stop to the progress of this growing evil except by the means of a navigable canal.*

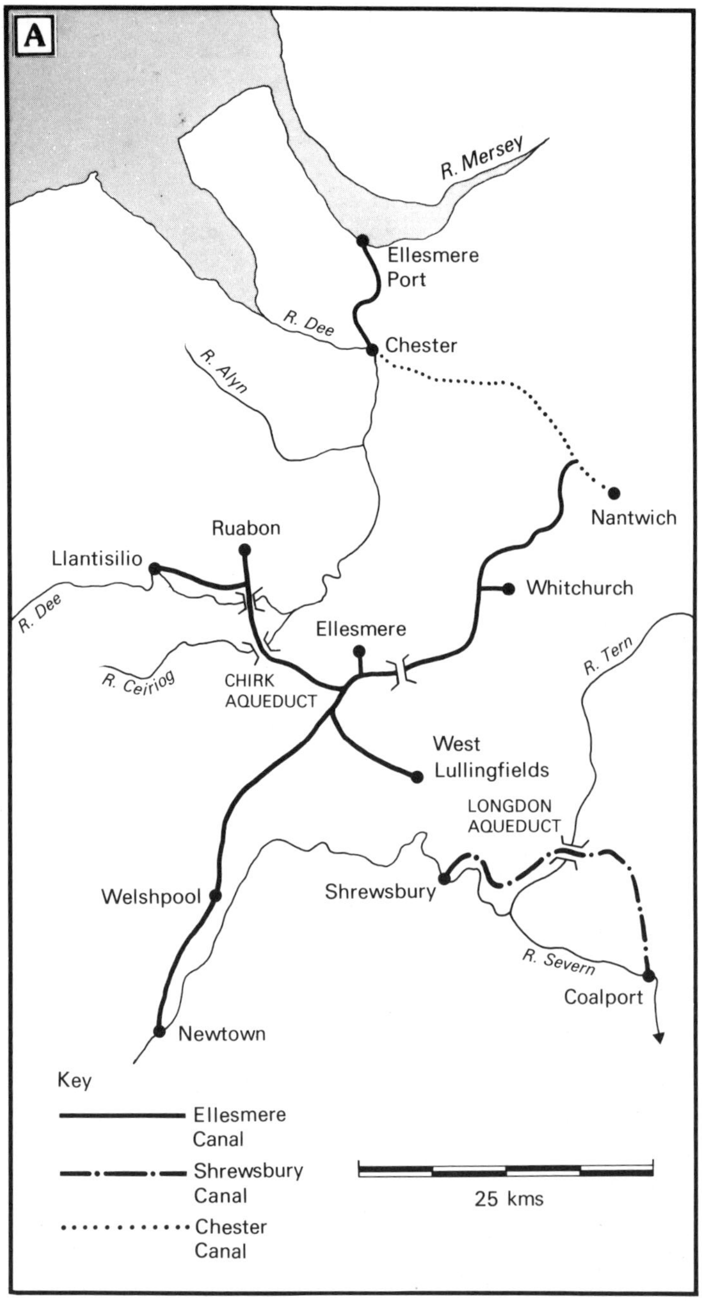

C

D

E

??????????????

1 The men who worked on the canal boats were called *bargees*. Often they and their families lived on the barges. Imagine you were travelling in 1800 on a boat from Oakengates to Shrewsbury. The journey took two days. Write a diary of your experiences. Mention:

life in the cabin; loading coals; going up the incline plane; the horse pulling the barge; passing up Eyton Locks; crossing Tern Aqueduct with its iron trough; passing over the turnpike road; The River Roden; pushing the barge through Haughmond Tunnel with your legs—legging; coming into Shrewsbury; arriving at the Castle Foregate Warehouse and unloading the coal.

2 Local Study. There should be a canal quite near your school. Try to find out as much as you can about it—when, why and how it was built, and how it changed the local area. Visit it and find out what original features are left e.g. locks and sluices, bridges, aqueducts, lockkeepers' houses, basins, warehouses.

3 Why was the Shrewsbury canal built? Use Telford's evidence to help you—**G**.

THE COMING OF THE RAILWAYS

A on page 46 shows an early wagon or tramway. In the background you can see iron furnaces. Wagonways were common in coal mining and iron-producing areas like this. By 1800 mine owners and iron masters used steam engines in their works (see pages 44-45). In 1804 an engineer, Richard Trevithick, fixed to a carriage a steam engine like the one in **B. A** is a picture of this first train. In 1808 Trevithick showed off his improved invention at Euston in London, **C.** From 1812 a few trains or locomotives began to be used on tramways in the north east of England. In 1813 a letter from a colliery owner said:

D *I shall have great pleasure in giving to his Grace the Duke of Portland, and also to you, every information that I can about the new way of pulling our coals by means of steam engines instead of horses.*

The engine which is used is thought to be of four horses' power of Trevithick's invention . . .

A

B

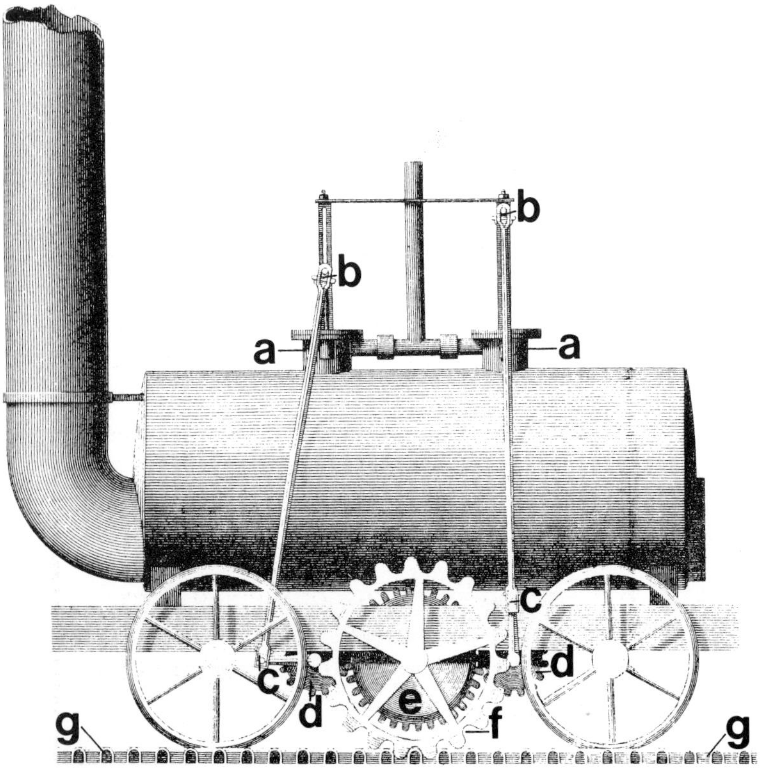

E *It is the most powerful one we have in use at present, and is made by Messrs Fenton, Murray & Wood of Leeds or any other engine builders, and cost £380 including £30 paid to Trevithick for his patent right. The experiments . . . have given the greatest satisfaction and promise to be attended with the most beneficial effects. It is supposed and indeed I think with a tolerable degree of correctness that five-sixths of the expense of leading the coals by horses will be saved by the invention, as I find it has cost us 2s (10p) per chaldron leading our coals to the river by horses, a distance of 5½ miles, while I am satisfied so soon as we get our own way completed to the river it will not cost us more than 4d (1½p) per chaldron conveying them by Mr Blenkinsop's way.*

Our loadings from that colliery are about 3600 chaldrons a year, we presume we shall save at least £3000 per annum at that concern . . . The results of our experiments at Kenton

have been that the engine is capable of drawing 16 full wagons each journey which we compute will weigh with the coals therein 64 tons, in addition to the weight of the engine (5 tons) . . .

Mr Blenkinsop, an engineer, invented the first usable locomotive in the coal-mining area of the North East. Another early engineer was George Stephenson. In 1814 he built his first steam engine, *Blucher*. Many others followed. Stephenson planned railways too. In 1825 he opened his Stockton and Darlington railway between Darlington and the port of Stockton. It was mainly used for transporting coal, but was the first public railway to use steam locomotives and to carry passengers. The railway age had begun.

??????????????????????????

1 How do you think Trevithick's engine, **B,** worked? The barrel is the engine's boiler. Mention how the following are linked:
a to **b, b** to **c, c** to **d, d** to **e, e** to **f, f** to the rails—**g,** which have notches in them.

2 Imagine you were present at scene **C.** Describe what you might see, hear and smell if you were to ride on the railway. Talk about the features **g, h, i, j, k** and **l.**

3 If you had to explain to the Duke of Portland why it would be worth buying a railway locomotive to use in his coal mines, draw up a list of the points you would make, using the evidence on this page and **E,** which is how letter **D** went on.

In your list mention:
a cost of the engine
b the saving in the cost of keeping horses
c ways it might be used
d possible problems (e.g. the weight of the engine on the old rails).

THE LIVERPOOL TO MANCHESTER RAILWAY

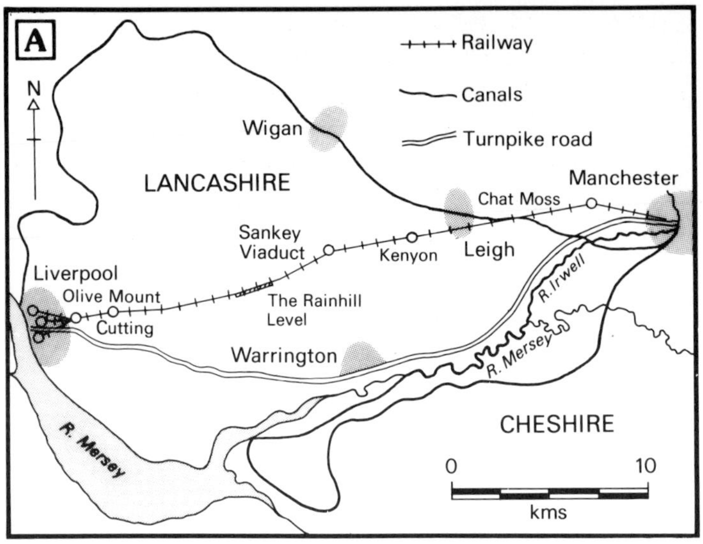

In 1824 a meeting of Liverpool's and Manchester's leading merchants and factory owners talked about their main problem. How were they to get raw cotton, cotton cloth and other goods quickly and cheaply between Liverpool and Manchester? The canals and turnpikes charged high prices, and the journey could take up to two days. After much talk the meeting decided to try to build a railway which would use locomotives. How could this be done?

First the merchants and industrialists had to get an Act through Parliament to allow them to build the railway. The Act would set up a railway company like a turnpike trust. The railway had many fierce enemies, and the Act took two years to get through Parliament. The Liverpool and Manchester Railway Company chose George Stephenson (see pages 26-27) to build their line. There were many problems for him to solve—especially how the railway would get across a huge marsh, Chatmoss.

A shows the canals and turnpikes, and the route of the railway. When it was almost built, the company had to choose a locomotive to pull its wagons and carriages. The company held a competition, **B,** on 1st October 1829 for the best engine, with a £500 prize for the winner. George Stephenson's son Robert won with his engine, the *Rocket* **C.** Using Stephenson's locomotives, the railway opened in 1830. The *Manchester Guardian*, a newspaper, described how a convoy of trains went from Liverpool to Manchester:

D 15th September 1830. *Rainhill Bridge was soon neared and the inclined plane of Sutton began to be climbed at a slower rate. The summit was soon gained, and twenty-four miles an hour became the maximum of the speed. At a*

B

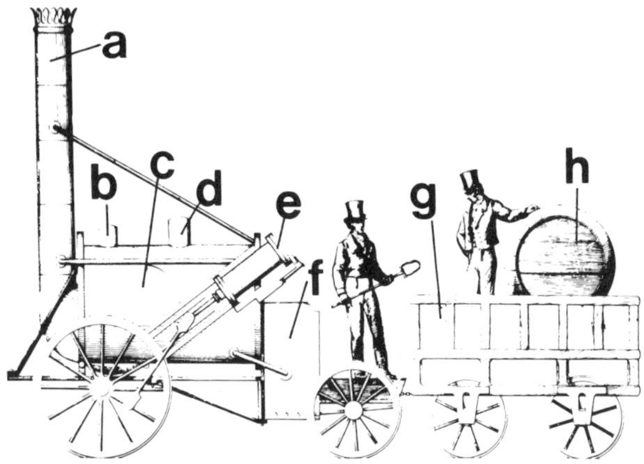

THE "ROCKET" OF MR ROBT STEPHENSON OF NEWCASTLE.

THE "NOVELTY" OF MESSRS BRAITHWAITE & ERRICSSON OF LONDON.

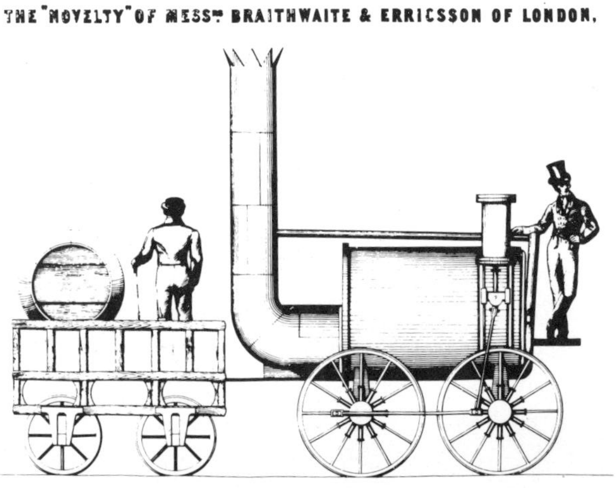

THE "SANSPAREIL" OF MR HACKWORTH OF DARLINGTON.

a chimney, **b** steamdome, **c** boiler, **d** safety valves, **e** cylinders, **f** firebox, **g** coal, **h** water barrel, **j** driving wheel.

quarter before twelve o'clock Sankey embankment and viaduct (**E**) *were in view, and here another brilliant group was assembled to greet the approach . . .*

The viaduct and embankment particularly held the Duke of Wellington's attention, and 'magnificent' 'stupendous' were heard frequently to issue from his lips. The viaduct was rapidly passed, and the engines . . . stopped to fill up with water and take in a fresh supply of fuel.

Here several gentlemen got down from the different carriages, and after walking on the railway for some moments, were preparing to return. Amongst the number was Mr Huskisson: he approached the Duke of Wellington. While in the act of shaking hands, herald sound announced the approach of the Rocket *engine, on the opposite rail. A cry of danger was instantly raised . . . The unfortunate man* (Huskisson) *became flurried, and rapidly caught hold of the door, but unhappily trying to climb he missed his footing, and either fell or was thrown by the door, and on falling to the ground, part of his person extended on the other rails, and* The Rocket *coming up at the instant went over his leg and thigh, and fractured* (broke) *them in a most dreadful manner.*

Huskisson, who was a famous MP, was the first man to die in a railway accident.

C

E **Sankey Viaduct**

? ? ? ? ? ? ? ? ? ? ? ?

1 Why do you think the railway had so many enemies?

2 Describe or draw the *Rocket,* showing how it worked; *or* as if you were a journalist present at the Rainhill trials, write a report saying why you think the *Rocket* won them.

3 Say what you might have thought, felt, seen, heard and smelled if you had travelled with the journalist on the first train from Liverpool to Manchester. Mention:

crossing the Rainhill Bridge; the train's amazing speed; meeting the Duke of Wellington; looking at the engine; seeing Mr Huskisson; sound of train approaching; panic; attempts to escape; fall; screaming; body removed; news of death.

4 What had led to the building of railways in 1830? As if you were talking to an early railway engineer, discuss:

a wagonways in mining areas;
b Trevithick's invention;
c early railways in the North East;
d the Stockton to Darlington railway;
e the problems facing the Liverpool to Manchester railway;
f Stephenson's work as an engineer – choice of route, the building of the railways, the stations;
g the competition to choose an engine;
h thoughts about the future of the railway.

THE SPREAD OF THE RAILWAYS, 1830-1900

Map **A** shows how the railways spread in the period 1830-1900. In 1886 a schoolboy wrote in his school magazine:

B *In England, more than in any country of Europe, lines or rails have spread themselves out in every direction over the land like the closely-spun fibres of a spider's web. Every pretty village must have its line and station, whether there are chances of it paying or not.*

C is more evidence about the work of the railway companies. **Railway Boom** shows how two companies might have competed to build lines in the region where you live. Such a contest happened in the area of map **A**, page 6.

??????????????

1 Draw a map of England to show how railways spread to link up the following:

cities—Birmingham, Sheffield, Manchester, Liverpool, Bristol, Leeds.

towns—Hull, Shrewsbury, Oldham, Rotherham.

villages—villages in your own area.

or draw such a map to show the spread of railways in your area to cities, towns and villages.

2 Use the evidence on this page, and pages 26-27, 28-29 to write a history of the spread of the railways. Mention:

early lines; build up of networks; rival companies; inventions; money invested; people employed; speed of spread of railways.

A

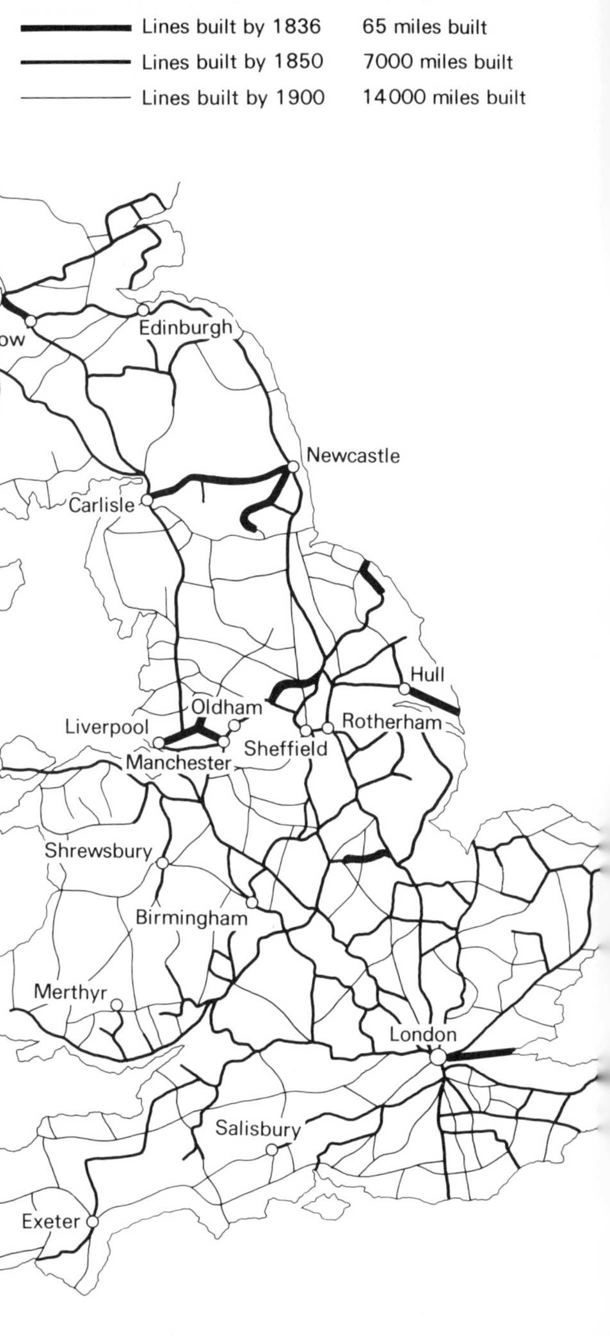

C **The Railway Industry, 1847 – 60**

	No. of navvies	Miles open	No. of railway workers	Money from goods/ passengers
1847	250 000	3 500	45 000	£ 8 million
1850	60 000	6 300	60 000	£13 million
1855	40 000	8 100	100 000	£21 million
1860	55 000	10 200	125 000	£28 million

RAILWAY BOOM

The map shows an area where two railway companies have just been started. They are based on cities **A** and **B.** The companies will build railways to as many towns and cities as possible. The company with the most lines will be the most successful.

How to play. The game is for two players. Take turns in your alphabetical order of surnames. e.g. Brown before Green.

Each round you can build *one* line from a city where you already have a line to any other *city* within sixty kilometres.

You *cannot* build a line to a city or town where there is a line of the other company.

When you have *built* lines to *all* the cities you can, you can begin to build them to the towns.

Each round you can build *one* line to a town from *any town or city* which is already part of your own rail network.

Keep a diary at the end of each round to say why you are building up your network in the way you are, and how successful you are in beating the rival company.

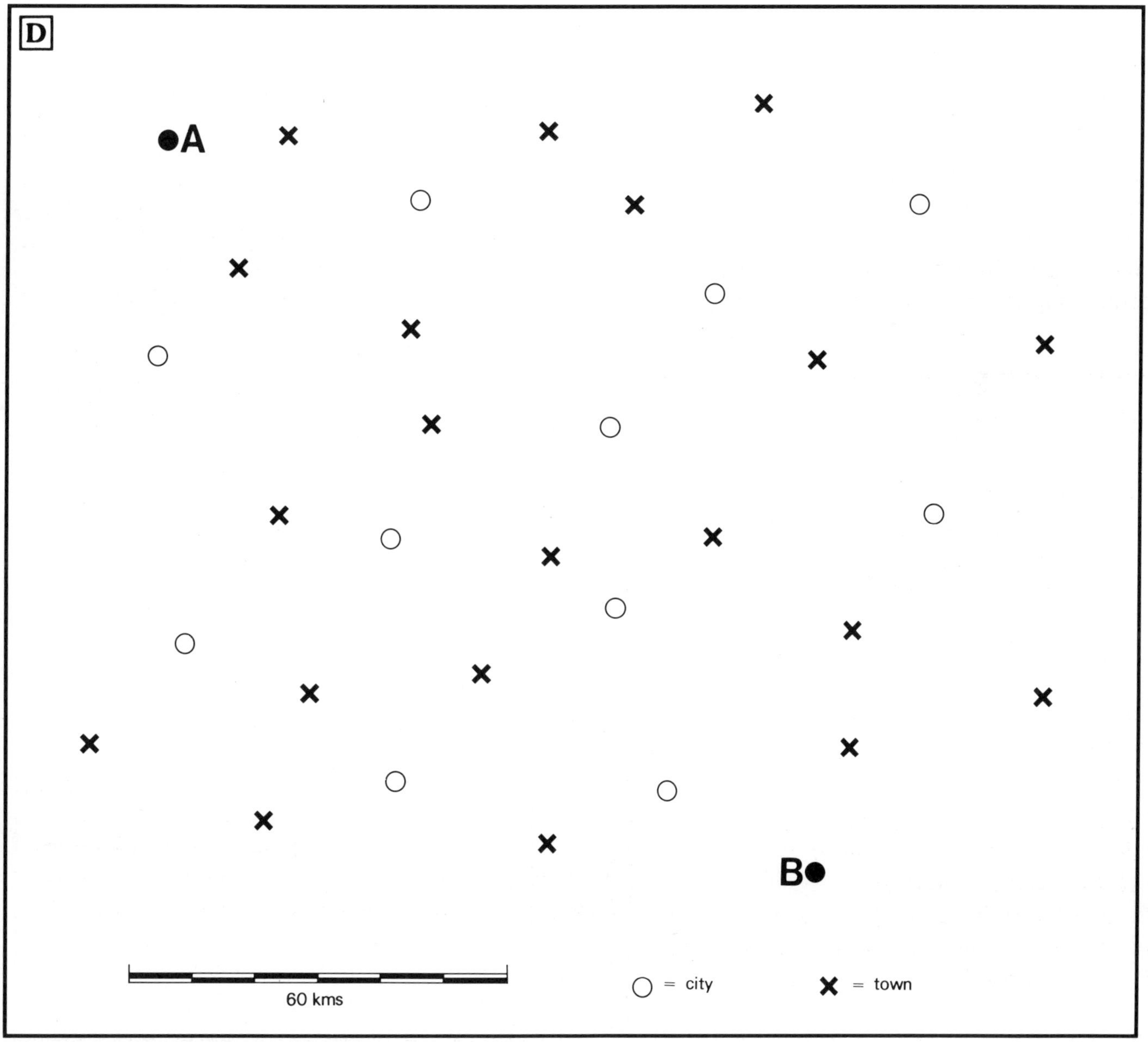

THE IMPACT OF THE RAILWAYS

A shows the impact of the railways upon Devon. A similar network would have grown up around where you lived. The 1866 schoolboy (see pages 30-31 **B**) carried on his story:

B *These numerous, badly thought out railways are for the most part as might be expected. It is a sad thing to be dragged slowly at the end of a long railway journey into any great English towns, and to see the woeful wilderness of criss-crossing lines become more and more intricate the further they penetrate among the streets. It is a melancholy thing to see all the dirty rubbish which always collects at a large station, to see the broken down outhouses, the ill-built sheds, the untidy signal boxes, the unsightly engine house, with here and there an old carriage with its wheels cut off, serving as a home for some hermit-like porter, and everything befouled with smoke and grime.*

The schoolboy would have passed through an area like **C.**

How might people who lived in and near your home have behaved when they heard that a

A

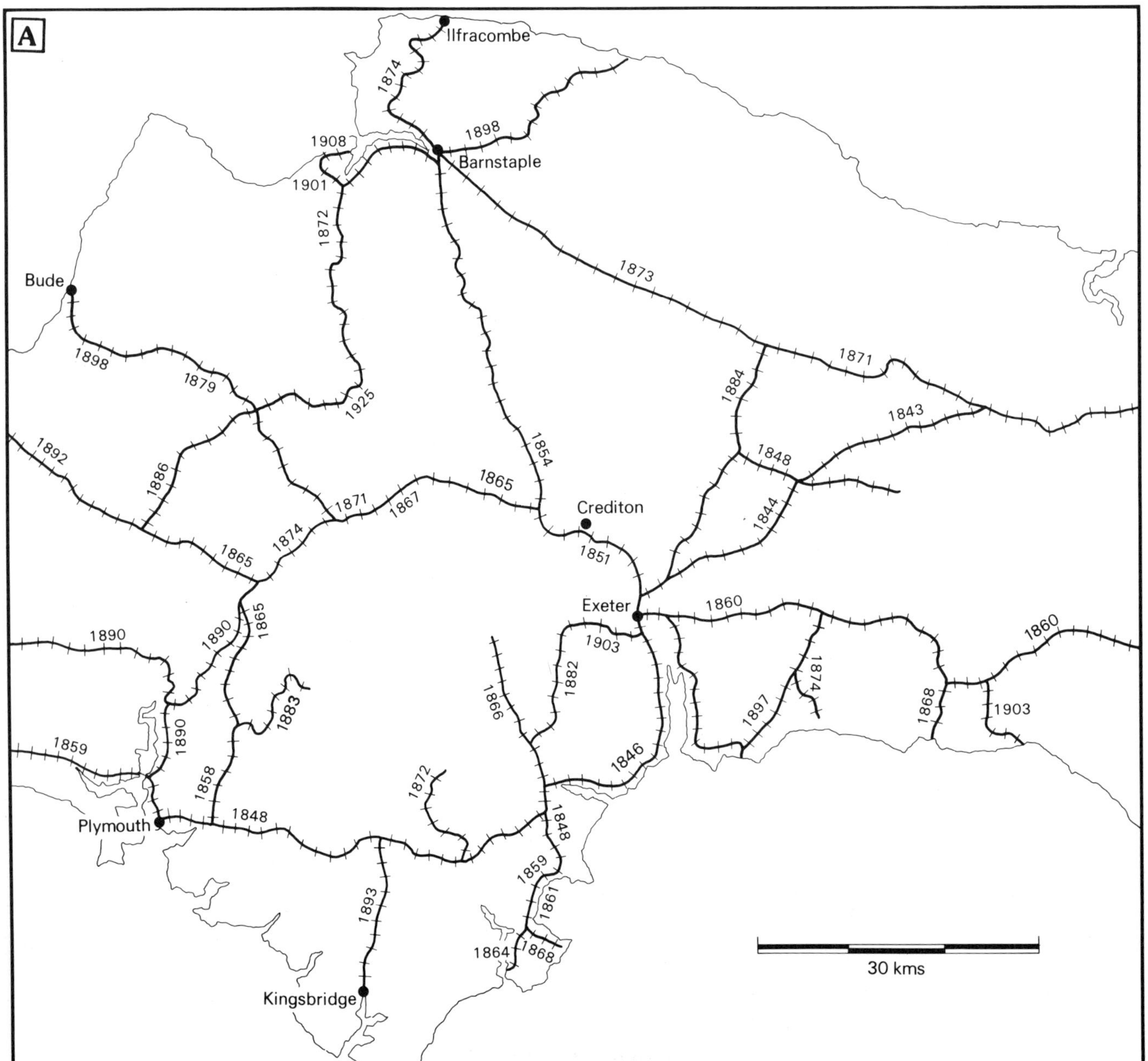

C

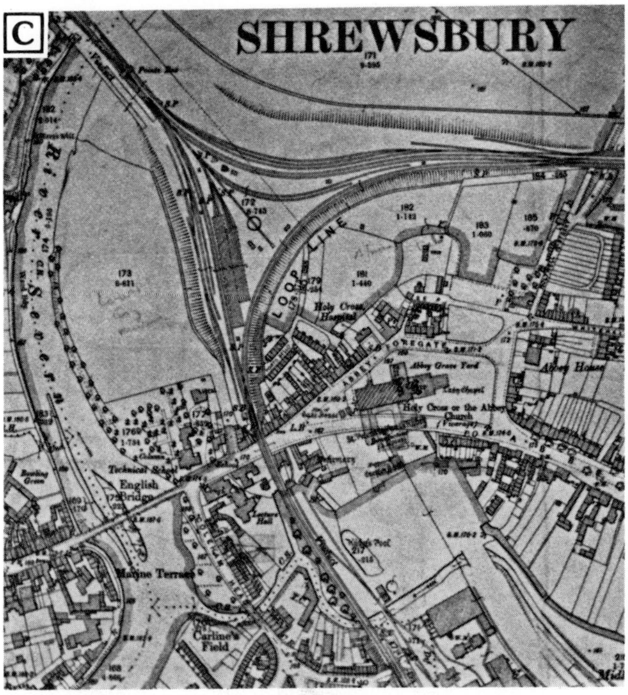

D

railway was being built through the area? In her novel *Middlemarch*, George Eliot wrote how people thought when they first heard of the coming of a railway.

E *Women both old and young regarded travelling by steam as dangerous, and argued against it by saying that nothing could induce them to get into a railway carriage. . . . But the slower wits . . . who occupied land of their own, their minds halted at the vivid idea of what it would be to cut the Big Pasture in two, and turn it into three cornered bits . . . 'The cows will all cast their calves, brother,' said Mrs Waule, in a tone of deep melancholy. 'If the railway comes across the Near Close I shouldn't wonder at the mare too, if she was in foal. It's a poor tale if a widow's property is to be spaded away, and the law says nothing to it.'*

A farm worker, Timothy Cooper, said why he was against the coming of the railway:

F *Ah! good for the big folks to make money out on . . . I'n seen lots of things turn up sin' I war a young un—the war an' the peace, an' the canells, an' the oald King George, an' the Regen' an' the new King George, an' the new un as has got a new name—an' it's been all aloike to poor men. What's the canells been t'him? They'n brought him neyther meat nor beacon, nor wage to lay by, if he didn't save it wi' clemmin his own insides. Times ha got wusser for him sin' I war a young 'un. An' so it'll be wi' the railroads. They'll only leave the poor men furder behind.'*

? ? ? ? ? ? ? ? ? ? ? ?

1 Travel Questionnaire

a When could you have first travelled to the following towns from London:
Crediton; Bude; Plymouth; Exeter; Barnstaple?

b When could you have first gone from Crediton to:
the seaside; a football match in Manchester?

c If you planned a trip from Ilfracombe to Kingsbridge in 1900, work out your shortest route.

2 Imagine you are living in your local town in 1840. Rumours are spreading like wildfire about the possible building of a railway. What might the following people have told you about their hopes and fears about the railway?

A local grain merchant: he buys grain from local farmers, which he mills and sells locally.

A publican: he runs the largest hotel in town, which is a stagecoach station. Carrier wagons stop to change horses here.

A smallholder: he owns a forty acre farm which is on the route of a possible railway.

A coal merchant: coal has been reaching him along the local turnpike road. The wagons are always breaking down, and destroying the road.

3 What impact did the railway have on area **C**?

4 How might railways have affected the following by 1880?
Holidays; spread of news; work; where people lived; trade; the look of towns.

THE NAVVIES

A *He had knee-straps around his knees, and a long strip of tin wedged between the straps and the legs of his moleskin trousers. He wore a peajacket and a gaudy kerchief wrapped around his neck. His white felt hat had an up-turned brim. But the waistcoat was the most noticeable. It was made of velvet, ornamented with large ivory buttons which ran down the front in double rows. The boots, which he called 'subs' were a different colour, shape and size.*

A is an eyewitness account of a navvy like **B.** Navvies like this built the network of roads, railways and canals which covered Britain by 1900 (see pages 30-31). **C** is what they looked like at work. They built bridges and aqueducts, and dug cuttings and tunnels. Near your school and home there will be examples of what they did.

B

C

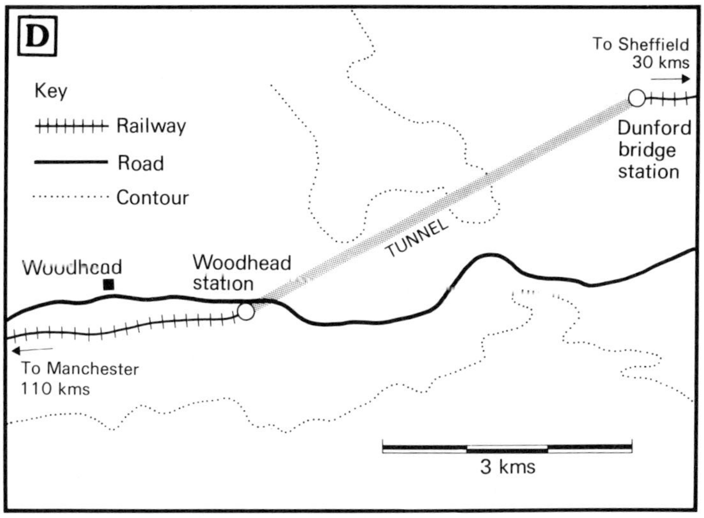

What were their lives like? In 1846 a group of MPs—a *Select Committee of the House of Commons*—looked at the living and working conditions of railway labourers. The MPs examined how navvies lived during the making of the Woodhead Tunnel which linked Lancashire's and Yorkshire's railways, **D** (see page 30). On 26th May 1846 Mr L. H. Pomfret gave his evidence to the committee. For six years he had worked part time as 'a surgeon upon the summit level of the Sheffield and Manchester Railway.' The committee asked him about accidents to navvies he had treated for injuries. He said:

E *I have the list in my pocket . . . which I will read to you.*

23 cases of compound fractures, including two cases of fractured skulls; 74 simple fractures; 140 severe cases, including burns from blasts, severe bruises, dislocations etc. One man lost both his eyes and one half of his foot.

Most of these accidents were connected with other injuries, for instance a man had his arm broken by a blast. The limb was much burnt, together with one eye and all that side of his head and face. There were several cases of broken ribs also among these cases. There have also been about 450 cases of minor accidents, including trapped and broken fingers, injuries to the feet and toes . . . Many of these minor accidents were caused by drinking and fighting.

Mr Pomfret did not see any of these accidents happen. He said that the men lived in hovels.

F *They were huts chiefly built by themselves, I think of loose stone and mud, and thatched with ling from the moors . . . I have attended several men that were hurt that slept in the boilerhouses or stables.*

Most navvies were paid every nine weeks, usually at a local public house or inn. For two or three days afterwards they would get drunk. Gangs of wild men roamed the country during these *randies*, fighting, stealing and wrecking. In February 1845 navvies working near Penrith in Cumbria rioted. Some 1200 made for the town of Penrith. A force of troops stopped them from attacking the town.

??????????????????????????

1 Use **A** to draw an *accurate* picture of a navvy.

2 Compare navvy **A**'s looks with those of a modern worker on a road building gang. Contrast their:
boots, trousers, shirts and waistcoat, hat, face and hands, how they work.

3 If you had been with Mr Pomfret on one of his visits to the Woodhead tunnel on the day after the men had been paid, say what you might have seen at the following places:
a one of the navvy's huts, where a man lay injured after an explosion in the tunnel.
b one of the stables, where a navvy was recovering from a broken arm and leg.
c the pub where the navvies had just been paid.
d a cutting like **C** where navvies were still at work.

4 Imagine you were at school in Penrith in February 1845 when news arrived that the navvies were marching on the town. Say what thoughts and feelings you might have had about them, and what they might do.

5 Discuss the reliability of Mr Pomfret's account as historical *evidence*.

THE TRANSPORT REVOLUTION!

CANAL BUILDER

Imagine you are a canal contractor like Telford. You have been asked to submit a plan for a canal from Molesbury to Nowkey. Mark on map **A**, page 21, your route and any of the following features you include. Put them in on the scale shown.

Tunnels Tunnels cost a lot of money—a kilometre of tunnel costs as much as ten kilometres of canal.

Aqueducts A canal can use an aqueduct to cross a stream or river.

Bridges The canal will be bridged where roads and tracks cross it.

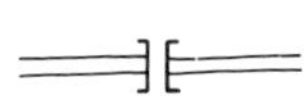

Wharves These will be built for loading and unloading where the canal crosses a turnpike road.

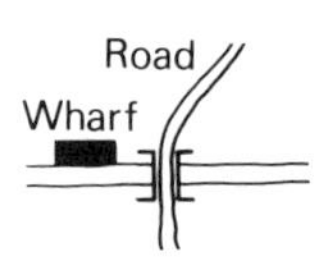

Locks You need these where the canal rises ten feet. It costs as much to build a lock as half a kilometre of flat canal.

Lock-keepers' house By every lock there will be a house for the lock-keeper, who takes tolls from the bargees who use the canal.

Basins Canal basins will be built near lock-keepers' houses. They allow barges to stop for the night, and to unload at wharves.

Bends The canal should be as short as possible and have no sharp bends.

Towpath Mark in a towpath for the horses who pull the barges along the canal.

Hand in a report with your canal plan. Give reasons for the features you have put in.

RAILWAY KING

It is 1835. Since the building of the Liverpool to Manchester railway there has been a railway boom. Rival firms have been formed to build lines between all the major cities of England. You belong to a company which wants to build a railway between Molesbury and Nowkey. At present they are linked by turnpike roads and the canal. The turnpike and canal companies, and major landowners, will probably be against your plans. They are afraid that railways will upset their farm animals, burn crops and ruin their estates. To gain support for a railway, you will need to produce a plan for its route, and say what advantages it will bring to the area. A public meeting will take place to discuss rival plans. At this you will have to defend the idea of a railway. Mark in your intended route on map **A**, page 21, with these features. Draw them in to the scale shown.

Straight route You should have only very slight bends.

Stations and stopping spots on routes. Site the station outside the towns so as not to upset the local people.

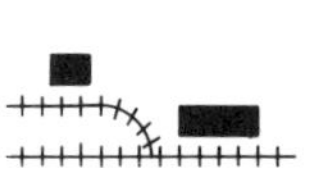

Bridges to cross streams, canals and turnpikes.

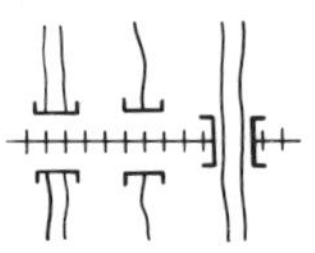

Cuttings and embankments where the railway climbs more than ten feet.

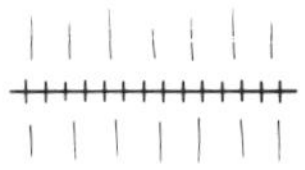

Tunnels where you are crossing a range of hills.

Also say what advantages the railway will bring the people of the area.

THE INDUSTRIAL REVOLUTION

THE ENVELOPE FACTORY

The Agricultural, Transport and Industrial Revolutions still affect our lives—where we live, what we eat, how we travel and the jobs we do. All around us we can see *evidence* of how Britain changed after 1740.

What was it like to set up an early factory? You can get an idea from making envelopes. To do this you will need a lot of scrap paper. You are a member of a team which has to make envelopes from sheets of this paper. There are up to four people in your team, which will plan how to do its own work. The team will be judged on *how many* (quantity) envelopes it makes, and *how good* (quality) they are. Follow the plan to make your envelopes.

Your team will make envelopes for *no more than five minutes.*

Stage 1 Make a square shape—fold along the diagonal. Cut off end.

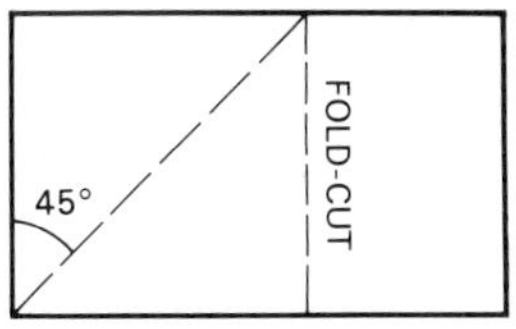

Stage 2 Fold corners 1 and 2 to reach the centre line of the diagonal.

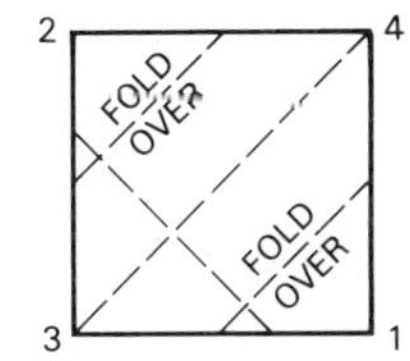

Stage 3 Fold corner 3 so that point reaches *well beyond* centre.

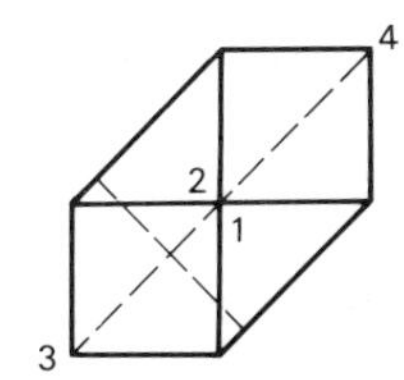

Stage 4 Fold point of flap 3 round and under points of flap 1 and 2.

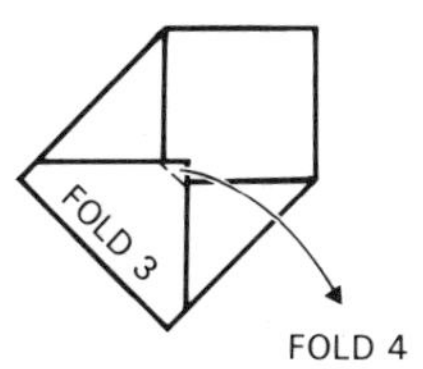

Stage 5 Fold final corner 4 so that point reaches *beyond* centre to make flap of envelope.

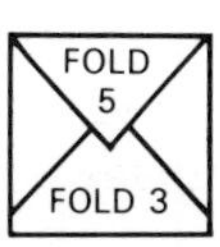

1 Write out each question below, with your answer chosen from the list.

a What raw materials did you need?
pencils, rubber bands, scrap paper, rawhide

b Where could you most easily make the envelopes?
factory, warehouse, open air, large room, small room, your home.

c What skills did you need?
mathematical, organisational, skilled fingers, none.

d What power did you need to make the envelopes?
electric, water, steam, human, nuclear, horse

e Who do you think might buy your envelopes?
family, friends, team members, shops, teachers

f Were more envelopes made by people working:
as individuals; in pairs; in threes; in fours?

g Were better quality envelopes made by people working:
as individuals; in pairs; in threes; in fours?

2 Describe the steps by which your team went about making its envelopes, and how successful you think you were.

3 What advantages do you think a factory has over people making the same kind of goods in their own homes?
(Work in homes is called *cottage industry.*)

COTTON: 1

The tourist's diary for 1790 said of his visit to the Peak District, Derbyshire:

A *Below Matlock a new creation of Sir Richard Arkwright's is started up, which has crowded the village of Cromford with cottages, supported by his three magnificent cotton mills. There is so much rock, so much population and so much wood that it looks like a Chinese town . . . . Speaking as a tourist these vales have lost all their beauties. The rural* (country) *cottage has given place to the lofty red mill and the grand houses of overseers. The stream, moved from its course by sluices and aqueducts, will no longer ripple and cascade. Every rural sound is sunk in the clamour of cotton works . . .*

B

B is a print of what the tourist saw. Richard Arkwright was the son of a barber. As a young man he was interested in machines. Thirty

D

Date	Nature of Spinning and Weaving	Bottleneck or Hold Up	Solution to the Problem
1730	Workers spun and wove raw cotton at home on spinning wheels and handlooms. Merchants paid them to do this, and sold their cloth.	Spinning and weaving by hand too slow to meet the increase in *demand* for cotton goods. Their import from India had made them very popular.	1733: Kay's *Flying Shuttle.* Kay was a weaver. He fixed a hammer to each side of his loom. This knocked the shuttle from side to side. This meant he could weave a wider cloth, and that the weaver could weave much more quickly.
1735–1770	Workers still spun and wove at home. The flying shuttle had doubled the speed of weaving.	Because of the increase in the speed of weaving, and the growth in demand for cotton cloth, the spinners were unable to spin enough thread for the weavers.	1763: Hargreaves invented the *Spinning Jenny.* This was a modified spinning wheel which could spin *eight* threads instead of *one.* 1769: Richard Arkwright invented the *Water Frame.* This used water power, and made much better thread than the Spinning Jenny. 1779: Crompton invented the *Mule*—see **E.** This combined the ideas of Hargreaves and Arkwright. It made a high quality thread.
1780–1810	The spinning of cotton was now carried on in *factories.* These were usually built on streams, and water powered the machines. Weavers still worked at home, although some cotton-spinning factories had sheds built for weavers to work in.	Demand for cotton cloth still growing. Water power could not be trusted all the year round. Weavers could not weave all the thread being made.	1781: Boulton and Watt (see pages 44-45) developed a *steam engine* which was easy to use in cotton factories. 1785: Cartwright patented a *power loom* for weaving cotton cloth. This meant cotton cloth could be now woven in factories. 1804: Horrocks improved the power loom. 1813: Roberts modified the power loom—they can now do work as good as hand-loom weavers.

E

years after Arkwright died, a Derbyshire writer tells us:

C *He got to know a clock maker of Warrington . . . to whom he seems to have given his ideas. With him he put together the first machine for spinning by means of rollers. . . . It was some time before he could get the help of money. . . . At length the famous Jerediah Strutt of Derby, who by the invention of the Derby rib was making a fortune from stocking manufacture . . . entered into parternship with him. In 1769, the first mill, upon Arkwright's ideas, was built at Nottingham. This was drawn by horses. In 1771 a second factory on a much larger scale was built at Cromford in this county, the machinery of which was turned by a water wheel.*

In the cotton industry, raw cotton was spun into thread. The thread was then woven into cloth. After the Industrial Revolution began, this spinning and weaving was done in factories. Hold-ups, or bottlenecks, slowed down the *industrialisation* of the cotton industry. Inventions helped get rid of the bottlenecks. **D** gives an idea of what happened, why, and when.

By 1820 cotton was woven and spun in steam-powered factories. Both *coal* and *water* were needed to make cotton. Lancashire was the centre of the cotton inudstry. Can you think why?

? ? ? ? ? ? ? ? ? ? ?

1 List the clothes you wear and what they are made of. How do you think they were made? How many are cotton?

2 Use picture **B** to continue the tourist's story, describing what the Cromford mill and its surroundings looked like.

3 Say how you think **E** worked, and what impact it had upon the earnings of a family that worked at spinning cotton with spinning wheels.

4 Write your own story of the life of Richard Arkwright, and the way in which he became a cotton king. Mention:

upbringing; inventions; help from Strutt; factories in Derby and Cromford.

COTTON: 2

A

If in 1840 you had visited three cotton factories at Hyde, Saltaire and Wilmslow, what might you have seen? **A** is a picture of such a factory. **B – D** are taken from reports and letters of the 1830s and 1840s.

B **At Hyde** *The head of the factory, Mr Thomas Ashton, has built himself a charming village in the midst of gardens and plantations, and on the other side of the road are two factories, sited between a torrent which supplies the engines with water, and two coal mines, which supply fuel.*

Mr T. Ashton employs 1500 work people of both sexes. One immense room, filled with looms, contains four hundred of them. . . . The houses lived in by the work people form long and large streets. Mr Ashton has built three hundred of them which he lets at 3s (15p) or 3s 6d (17p) per week. Each house contains upon the ground floor a sitting room, a kitchen and a back yard, and above are two or three bedrooms.

C **At Saltaire** *The spinning factory . . . includes six storeys, and is cut in the centre by the engine house, containing four gigantic steam engines, nominally of 400 horse power, but really the strength of 1200. The spinning factory is built on the most massive style, the walls in thickness rivalling the Norman keeps of old, and supported by arches standing on iron pillars and covered by a cast iron roof, making the building consequently fireproof.*

Running at right angles to the spinning house is a pile of buildings seven storeys high and 350 yards long, used as warehouses. . . . On each

E

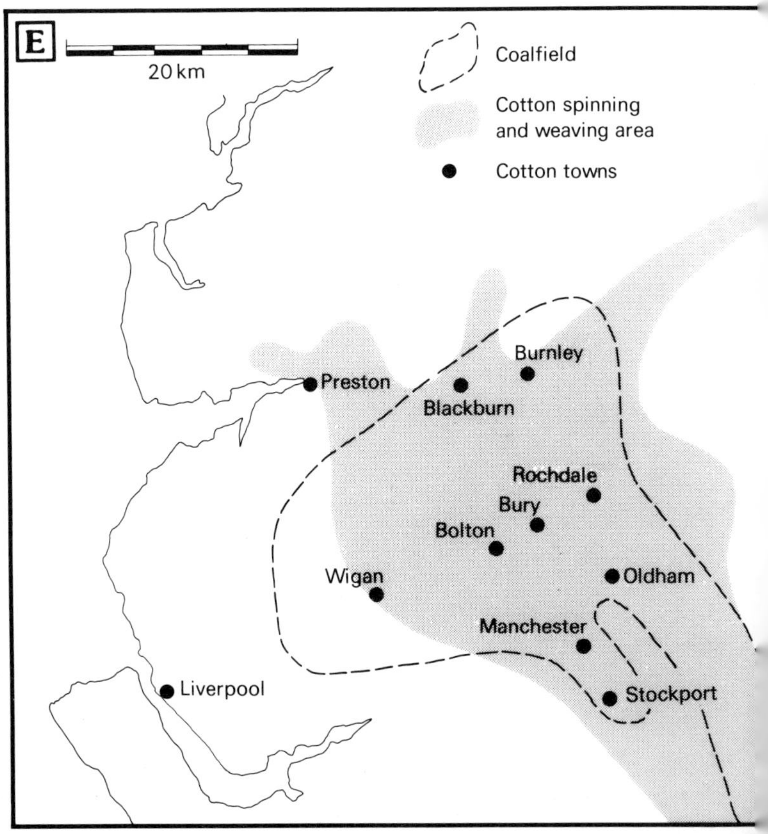

F The number of mills in Manchester

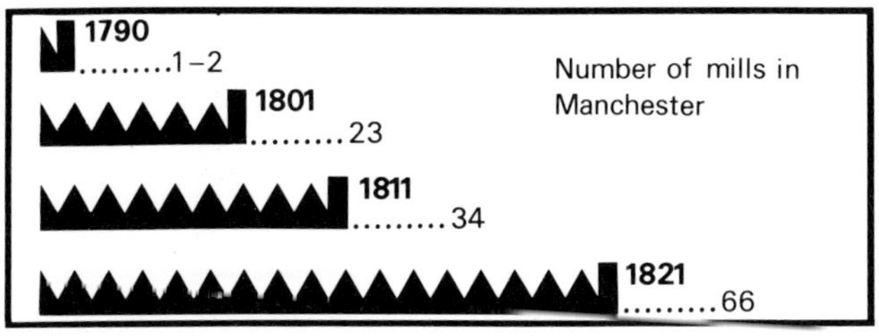

side of the warehouses the ground is occupied with (used for) *the preparing and weaving sheds . . . The dwelling houses are . . . well supplied with good water and also with gas from the gasometer at Saltaire works, which is capable of yielding gas for 5000 lights.*

D At Wilmslow *At a little distance from the factory, on a sunny bank, stands a handsome house, two storeys high, built for the accommodation of the female apprentices. Here are well fed, educated and lodged, under kind supervision, sixty young girls.*

The main area for the cotton industry was Lancashire—see **E. F** shows the increase in mills in Manchester. **G** and **H** give an idea of the growth of the textile industry—cotton, wool, linen and silk.

H The growth of the textile industry

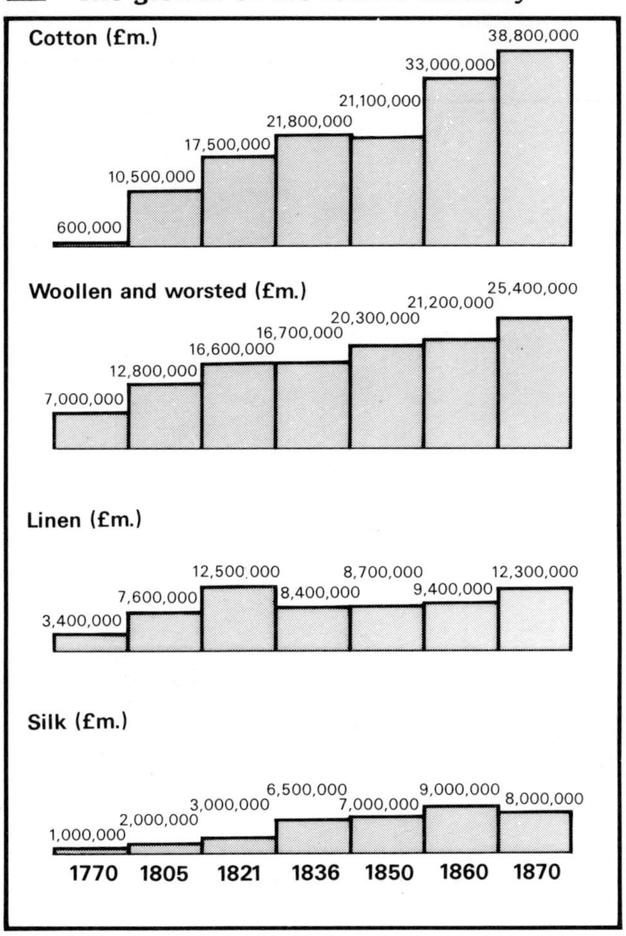

G Amount of cloth made, 1770-1872

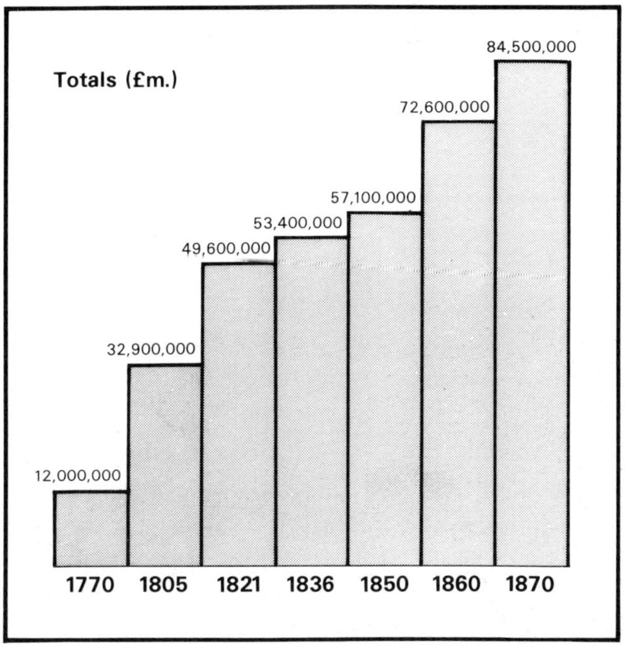

1 Use **A** and **B** to draw a map of what you think the Hyde factory and houses might have been like.

2 What might a visitor in 1849 say about the following on a visit to a cotton spinning and weaving area:

a the mill owner's house;
b the houses built for the workers (see pages 56-57);
c the inside of a spinning factory and weaving mill;
d the use of steam engines (see pages 44-45);
e the supply of water for factory and homes;
f the supply of gas?

3 Say why the Hyde, Saltaire and Wilmslow factories and cotton towns might have been planned in the ways described.

4 Plot on a line graph the growth of the textile industry's output from 1770-1872, and the increase in the value of cotton and wool manufacture.

5 Use this information and the rest of the evidence on this page, and what else you can find, to write a history of the textile industry during the industrial revolution.

COTTON MASTER!

Imagine it is 1782, and you own a silk works. How much money might you make as a cotton master? You and your partner have decided to set up a factory for spinning cotton thread. Before, you owned a silk factory. A fall in silk prices means that you are now making a loss. There is a boom in demand for cheap cotton cloth. It is spun in factories. Weavers weave the thread into cloth in their homes. Map **A** shows possible sites—A, B, C, and D—for your cotton spinning mill. Map **A** is of Area 4 on page 6. In picking a site for your cotton factory, think about points **a** – **c.**

a The factory should be close to a road. This will make it easy to get the raw cotton to the mill, to send the thread to the weavers, and to collect the woven cloth.
b It should be close to the town where the factory workers will live. They are the labour force necessary to work the machinery.
c It should be on one of the streams which will turn the spinning machines. Water power is vital for the factory's success.

To choose where to site your spinning mill, make out a table like the one below. For *each* point **a** – **c,** tick *one* site you would choose. For example, for point **a** you might choose site D. So tick D.

Choice of mill site				
Site	A	B	C	D
Points **a**				
b				
c				

Class choice	
Site	Numbers choosing
A	
B	
C	
D	

Diary Start a diary of your career as a cotton master. Mention:
silk factory; problems; sites for cotton factory; advantages and disadvantages; reasons for your choice.

A

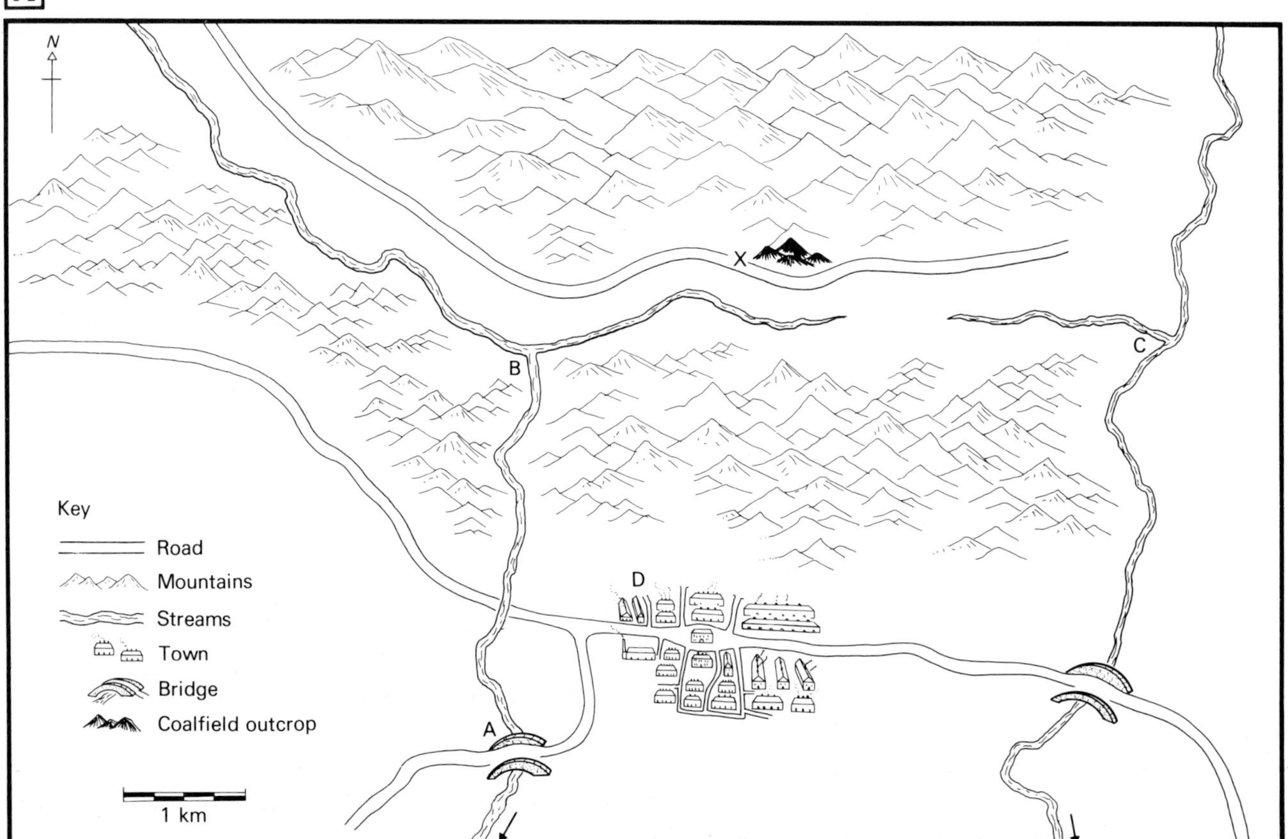

Imagine it is 1790. You and your partner built your cotton factory in 1782, and have made enough money to pay for its building and machines—£2500. The factory contains 20 *water frames*. They can be used easily in a factory—unlike Hargreaves' Spinning Jenny. You and your partner have to decide how much cloth to make for the coming year. Think about points **d – f.**

d You need five people to work a water frame. You pay each one £20 a year in wages—a total of £100 for each water frame.
e The raw cotton from America for spinning into thread (see pages 38-39) will cost you another £100 a year for each water frame used.
f You employ one weaver to weave the thread from each water frame into cloth. His wages are £50 a year.

The problem is, how much cotton should you spin? There could be a *fall in demand*—people might not buy the cloth you make. A revolution has just broken out in France, and there is a war in Europe. For the factory to work efficiently—that is, make most money—you will need to use all of its machinery and sell everything it makes.

You can also spend up to £1000 trying to improve the working of the water frames. All the time other cotton masters are improving the thread they make. A better quality thread or yarn could help you to sell *much more* cloth, and to get a *higher price*.

Copy out table **B,** and put in what you decide to do.

B

Cost of making cloth 1790

Cotton for each water frame used, at £100 each	£______
Wages for each water frame used, at £100 each	£______
Wages for a weaver for thread from each water frame, at £50 for each weaver	£______
Amount spent on inventions	£______
Total costs for year	£______

Income from selling cloth 1790

Total amount of cloth sold, ______ (number of bales) ______ (price for each bale). This depends upon its quality. No. of bales × prices = income for the year.

Income for year	£______
Less *total costs for year*	£______
Profit for 1790	£______

Diary Carry on your diary, and say how you took your decisions about making cloth and spending on inventions in 1790, and how well your firm did in that year.

Imagine it is 1845. On map **A**, X shows the site of a new factory and cotton town you intend to build. The new site is near the coal mines, which will provide fuel for the steam engines. They will power the spinning and weaving machines. Use the evidence on pages 38-41 to plan your own cotton town. Draw the following features in on the scale shown:

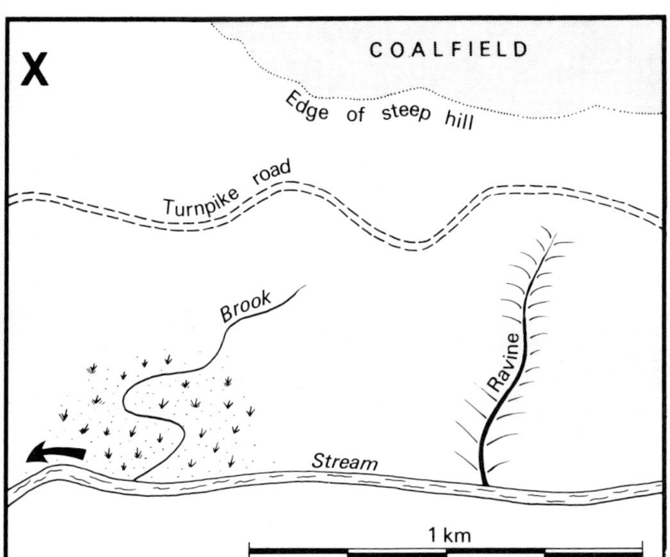

spinning factory — Spinning mill

weaving factory — Weaving factory

gas works — G

warehouses — Warehouse

roads and tracks

apprentices' houses (boys and girls) — Boys — Girls

coal mines (3)

houses for three hundred families — Ten houses

factory owner's mansion — Mansion

Diary Make an entry in your diary, giving *in full* the reasons for *each* of your choices in your plan.

STEAM POWER - THE STEAM ENGINE

William Reynolds (see pages 48-49) was delighted. Plans for a new steam engine were going well. On 1st April 1790 he scribbled a letter to a friend:

A *It is an entire new engine which I think very good for use in a coal mine as being I believe less expensive to build, better for removal from one place to another and one which will take less fuel to produce the same effect than any before invented . . . It is yet quite secret and if as good a thing as I believe it, will replace Boulton & Watts . . . If thy friends can wait a while I think they had better.*

Since 1712 steam engines had been used in mines. At first they were expensive to build and run, and did not work well. These early Newcomen steam engines kept the same design until about 1760, **B,** although they became much larger. In the 1760s two changes greatly improved the steam engine. An ironmaster, John Wilkinson, invented a machine for boring accurate cylinders, and in 1769 James Watt invented a much improved steam engine, **C.** Inventors soon did a lot more work on the steam engine, and by 1800 small high-pressure engines were able to move carts, railway engines and boats.

James Watt built most of the steam engines which were used in mines, iron works and factories. From 1800 they became the most common source of power in industry. This meant that factories no longer had to be built on streams and rivers. They needed coal now, and coalfields became the new centres of industry, as in the wool industry of Yorkshire and the cotton industry of Lancashire—see **D** and **E.**

Newcomen's steam pump, 1711

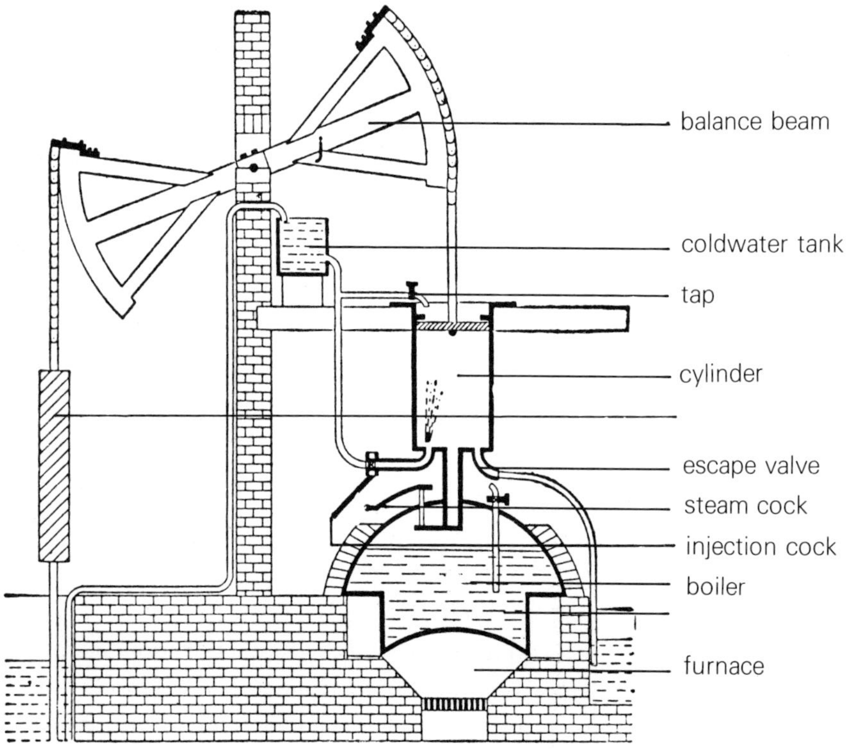

How Newcomen's engine worked: 1. Steam cock opened to let steam into cylinder as counter-weight raised piston, then closed. **2.** Injection cock opened to let cold water into cylinder, condensing steam and producing a vacuum, so that air pressure pushed piston down.

C **Watt's single-acting engine, 1775** (Boiler omitted)

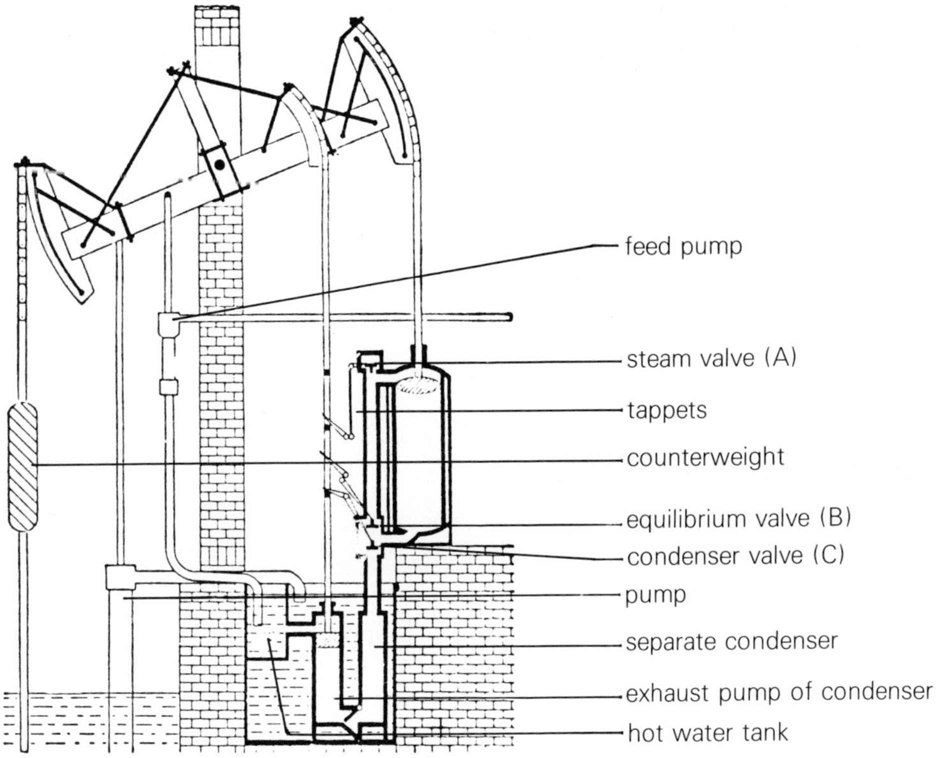

How Watt's engine worked: 1. Steam valve A and condenser valve C opened, making vacuum below piston and letting in steam above, causing piston to push down. **2.** At end of downstroke, valve B opened, so that counterweight pulled piston up and steam flowed round under piston. Then valve B is shut, and **1** was repeated.

D **Steam engines set up, 1775-1800**

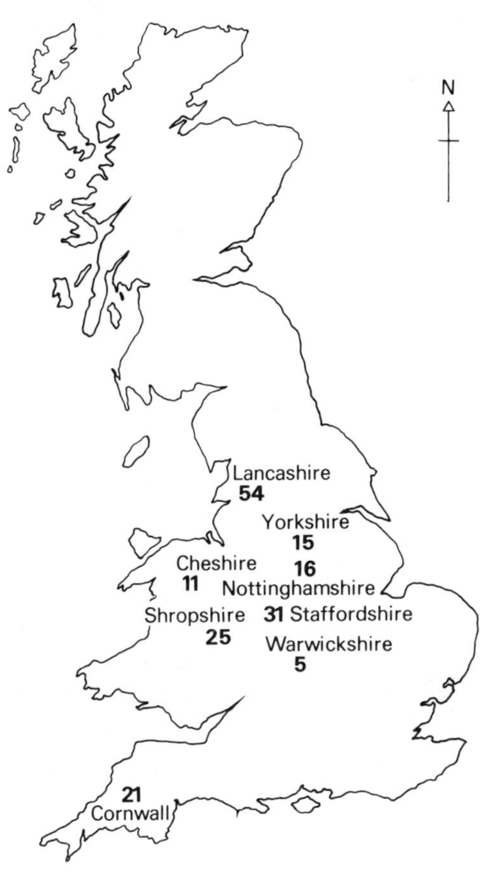

E **Industries using steam engines by 1800**

Cotton mills	84
Coal mines	30
Iron works	28
Copper mines	22
Canals	18
Breweries	12
Wool mills	9

????????????

1 **a** What kinds of industry used steam engines by 1800?
b Why do you think these industries had given up using water power?

2 If you had received letter **A,** list the advantages which his steam engine might offer your coal works.

3 Either draw *or* describe the Newcomen engine, to show how it worked. Do a similar drawing or description of the Boulton & Watt engine to show in *what way it was better* than the Newcomen engine.

IRON

1758. The artist finished his picture, **A**, of the ironworks, furnace pool and houses of Coalbrookdale, Shropshire. Coalbrookdale was then the centre of the world's biggest iron-making area. What clues does the picture give us about the making of iron in 1758? How had iron production changed in the previous fifty years?

The Darby family owned the ironworks in **A**. Since 1709 they had begun to use *coal* instead of *charcoal* (made from wood) in their furnaces to smelt ironstone into *iron*. Point **a** on **A** shows where *coal* is being turned into *coke* for the use in furnaces. Coal could not be used straight from the ground, as it had chemicals in it which ruined the iron. By turning it into coke these impurities were burnt off. Coal mines surrounded the Coalbrookdale works—**B**. To make iron the Darbys also had to have limestone and ironstone, see **B. C** is a modern drawing of the old furnace at Coalbrookdale.

Iron from the furnaces was cast into moulds to make *pigs* of cast iron, or goods such as pots and pans and iron beams and girders.

To make goods like knives and forks *cast iron* had to be beaten and hammered in a forge to turn it into *wrought iron*. Ironmasters tried all the time to improve ways of making cast and wrought iron (or *steel*). **D** shows the most important of their inventions.

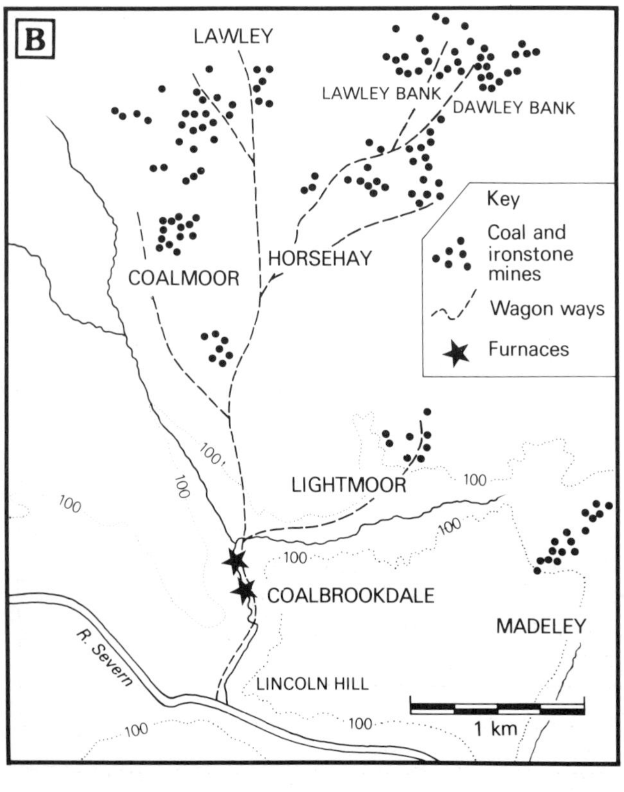

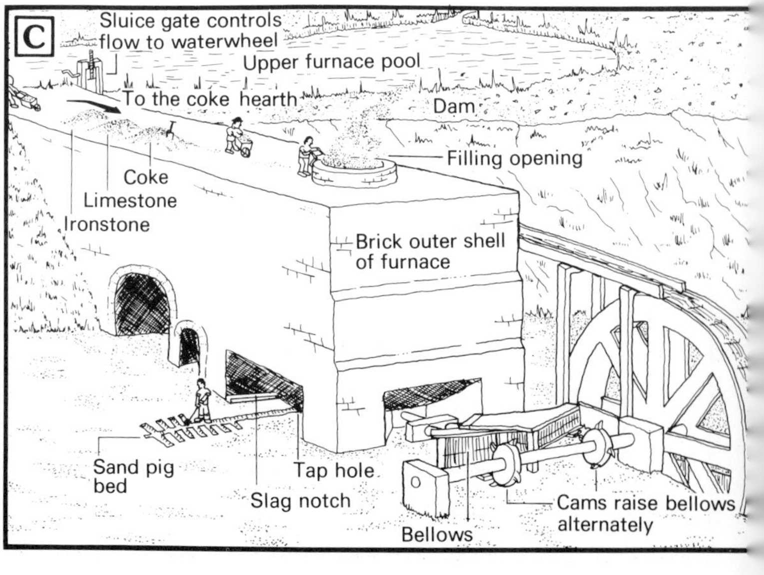

D Date	Invention	Consequences
1709	Smelting by Coke Darby inventor	Used coke instead of charcoal for smelting iron.
1740s	Huntsman's Process	Used coke to produce high quality cast steel. Needed high quality ore, so little used.
1766	Reverbatory Furnace	Helped produce higher quality iron from coke furnaces—but very expensive to run.
1775	Steam Engine used to work furnace bellows	Furnaces much more efficient, and no longer relied on water power for working.
1783	Cort's Puddling and Rolling Process	Turned cast-iron from coke furnaces into wrought-iron suitable for making tools etc. cheaply and easily. End of coke smelting except for high grade steel.

Before the 1760s ironmasters used water wheels to power the bellows which blew air into their furnaces, and which worked the hammers and machines in the forge. This was a problem, because the water did not always flow at the same speed or level. The steam engine solved this difficulty. They were in common use in ironworks by the 1790s.

From 1800-1900 there were many changes in the making of iron and steel. In 1885 Henry Bessemer discovered how to make large amounts of cheap steel in his converter. In 1867 William Siemen's open hearth allowed British ironmasters to use local poor grade coal, iron ore and scarp iron to make steel.

??????????????????????????

1 Either draw a diagram *or* say how a knife would have been made in 1790. Show:
raw materials; making coke; furnace process; forging steel; making knife.

2 Say what advantages came from the following changes in the making of iron:
- **a** coke instead of charcoal;
- **b** steam engines instead of water power;
- **c** Cort's puddling process;
- **d** Neilson's hot blast;
- **e** Bessemer's converter;
- **f** Siemen's open hearth method.

3 Let us travel back in time to 1760. Pretend you are an adviser to an ironmaster, Richard Reynolds, William's father (see pages 48-49). Richard has decided to build a new furnace in Area 4, pp 6, 49 **F**. A problem is whether to use *charcoal* or the new *coke* to smelt the iron. To help Richard, you have to make out a table like **E** below. For each point, give a mark out of five, with high marks in favour and low marks against. Add up the marks. Choose the method with the highest total.

4 Use the evidence on these pages to write your own history of the iron industry from 1740 to 1900.

E	Charcoal	Mark	Coke	Mark
1	You know how to make charcoal and your workers are happy to use it. There is still plenty of woodland nearby for you to get all the charcoal you need.		Coke can be made easily all the year round. A charcoal furnace can only work for six months because of the difficulty in getting enough charcoal to last a year. It needs huge areas of woodland to make enough charcoal. Soon it will begin to run out.	
2	The iron from a charcoal furnace is of very high quality—and sells for a high price. It can be used to make wrought iron, like knives and ploughs.		Although the iron from a coke furnace can only be used at present for making cast iron goods like pots, you hope soon to improve the quality. Also, a coke furnace will make about one third more iron than a charcoal furnace.	
3	Because at present you can send your charcoal by barge down the river, see **B,** you can have your forge and furnace close together.		Your coke furnace and forge can be next to one another. Raw materials—coal, ironstone and limestone—can easily reach the furnace from the local mines.	
	Total for charcoal		**Total for coke**	

THE IRONMASTER: WILLIAM REYNOLDS (1758-1803)

A March day in 1803. The mourners stood round the grave in the Quaker burial ground at Coalbrookdale. They were at the funeral of William Reynolds, one of the great ironmasters. He had been a member—partner—of the Darbys of Coalbrookdale. In 1880 John Randall, a local historian of Coalbrookdale, wrote what he had found out about William Reynolds. When iron workers were thrown out of work during a depression William used to give them soup three times a week. John Randall tells the story of how:

A *A number of men thrown out of employ* (work) *came to him in a body for relief* (help) *during a deep snow. He set them to clear an entire field, and to make him a snow-stack, which they did, of large proportions* (size), *receiving daily wages for the same.*

William always liked a joke. One tale Randall heard was about 'Sniggy Oakes'. William Reynolds let Sniggy live in a house rent free by the River Severn. Sniggy's only payment was to ferry William across the river in his boat when William wanted him to. The nearest bridge was two miles away.

B *One evening, Sniggy, knowing he was out on the other side, went to bed instead of sitting up, which he found a deal more comfortable on a cold wet night. Mr Reynolds, after calling him first one name and then another . . . and changing it for 'Boat! boat! ferry! ferry!' had to go round by the bridge. Coming opposite the cottage where Sniggy was snug in bed, he smashed every window, shouting 'Boat!' at every blow of his huge stick.*

William Reynolds loved to carry out experiments in his ironworks, (see page 47) and was very interested in science. His ironworks were the most modern in Britain. In 1799 he was worried that Swedish iron was much better than his own. John Randall wrote:

E **The inclined plane which hauled barges from a low canal to a high one.**

F

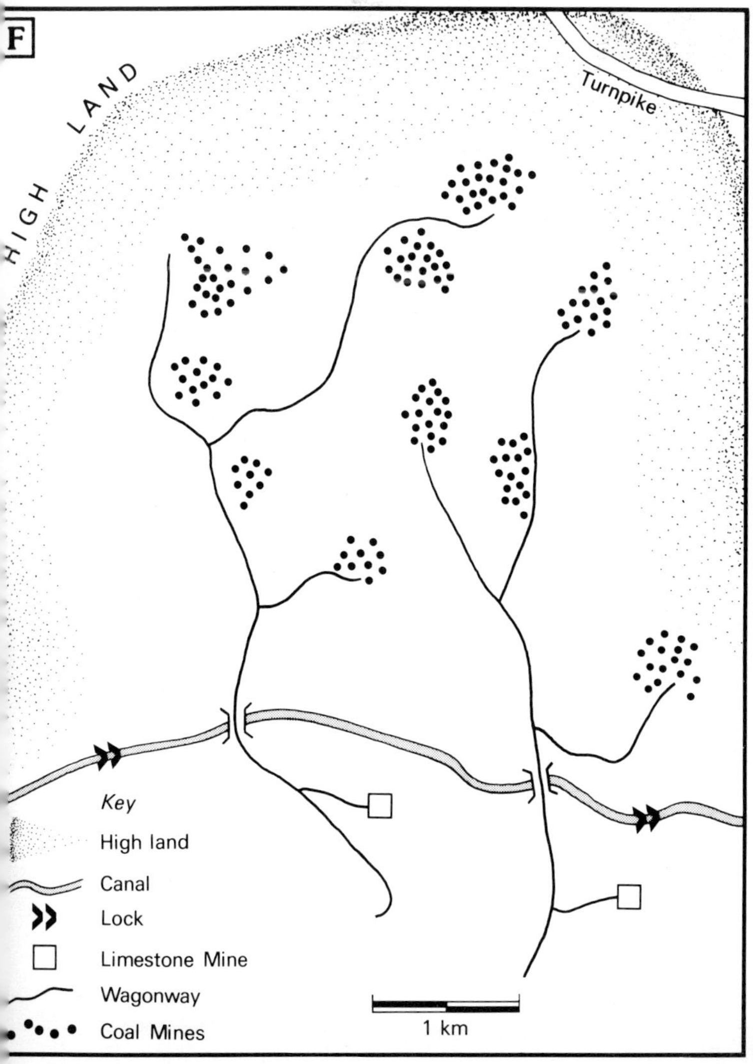

C *Mr Reynolds thought he saw how to produce metal equal to that made from magnetic and richer ores of the Swedish and Siberian mines when Bergam (a scientist) published his analysis of Swedish iron, showing the large amount of manganese it contained.*

William Reynolds tried to find out about all sides of the iron and engineering industry.

D *Nothing in fact was known about iron ore, iron making and machinery but what he knew or else took steps to acquaint himself with, if he had the opportunity. We have a number of large foolscap Mss* (hand written manuscripts) *volumes of experiments and extracts neatly copied, with pen and ink drawing of machines, parts of machines etc., showing that whilst Smeaton and Watt* (see pages 44-45) *were busy in perfecting the steam engine, Mr Reynolds was trying to apply it to purposes similar to those to which it is now applied as a locomotive.*

Thus he constructed a locomotive with a wagon attached, the cylinder and boiler of which are still preserved. An accident, we believe a fatal one, which happened to one of the men upon starting the engine, led Mr Reynolds to abondon the machine: but he by no means lost faith in the invention. On the contrary, he used to say to his nephew 'I may never live to see the time, but thee may, when towns will be lighted by gas instead of oil and candles, when vessels will be driven without sails, and when carriages will travel without horses.'

The most famous of William's many inventions was the inclined plane, **E**.

? ?

1 When William Reynolds died in 1803, the story of his life, an *obituary*, was printed in the newspapers. From the evidence on these pages write such an obituary for him. Describe:
—how he treated out of work men;
—his sense of humour and fair play;
—his use of science;
—his inventions, e.g. steam locomotive, inclined plane;
—what he knew about iron-making;
—why he was a success as an ironmaster.

2 How do you think William tried to improve his iron after reading the scientific report about the making of Swedish iron?

3 By 1800 iron-making was greatly increasing. Imagine you were advising an ironmaster about where to build a new furnace on map **F**—Area 4 of map **A** on pages 6-7. Where would you advise the ironmaster to put it? It will have to be:
a near a group of ironstone and coal mines;
b downhill from them so that wagons can freewheel down to the furnace;
c close to the canal so that iron can be sent to market;
d close to the limestone quarries.

4 Why do you think we can trust John Randall's evidence about William Reynolds?

WORK IN THE COAL MINE

C

In July 1825 the government list of sudden deaths in Shropshire states:

A *Jn Roberts working engine at coalpit, engine crushed him at Dawley Green . . . Jas Harvey working at coalpit, fell to bottom at Dawley, Parish Wellington. Rd Pritchard working in coalpit, coal fell on him, Parish Dawley. Rd Sheppard working in coalpit, damp took fire at Horse Hays, Parish Dawley.*

What was it like to work in such mines, where so many died? In 1842 a group of MPs formed a *parliamentary commission of enquiry* to look at how people worked in the mines. 37-year-old Betty Harris told the MPs:

B *I was married at 23, and went into a colliery when I was married . . . can neither read nor write.*

I work for Andrew Knowles of Little Bolton (Lancashire) and make sometimes 7s (35p) a week, sometimes not so much. I am a drawer, and work from 6 in the morning to 6 at night. Stop about an hour at noon to eat my dinner: have bread and butter for dinner: I get no drink. I have two children, but they are too young to work. I worked at drawing when I was in the family way. I know a woman who has gone home and washed herself, taken to her bed, been delivered of a child and gone to work again under the week.

I have a belt around my waist, and a chain passing between my legs, and I go on my hands and feet. The road is very steep, and we have to hold by a rope, and when there is no rope, by anything we can catch hold of. There are six women and about six boys and girls in the pit I work in: it is very hard work for a woman. The pit is very wet where I work, and the water comes over our clog-tops always, and I have seen it up to my thighs. It rains in at the roof terribly. My clothes are wet through almost all day long. I never was ill in my life, but when I was lying in.

C shows women workers like Betty. She told the MPs that:

D *I am very tired when I get home at night. I fall asleep sometimes before I get washed. I am*

F

not so strong as I was, and cannot stand my work so well as I used to. I have drawn till the skin was off me: the belt and chain is worse when we are in the family way. My feller has beaten me many a time for not being ready. I were not used to it at first, and had little patience.

What might you have seen at the bottom of a coal mine in 1842? A visitor said:

E *What a wild, gloomy and strange scene! A black cavern of immense extent was before me, shown by a few glimmering lights. We went on a good way, when suddenly I saw two rows of lights burning, one on the right, the other on the left. These were the lights by which the colliers were at work getting the coal.*

F is a drawing of a miner. The account went on:

G *Here the poor fellows sit on the ground with their sharp picks undermining a certain quantity of the coal measured and marked out with chalk. . . . Then comes the hammer-man with his hammer, and driving his wedge in above, down comes the mass of coal . . . As the poor fellows clear away the coal, they prop up the roof with pieces of wood.*

Children also worked in the mines (**H**)—drawing sledges and carts with coal on them, or opening and shutting trap doors.

H

????????????????????????

1 What kinds of accidents do you think miner **F** might have at work?

2 Describe the scenes in **C**, and say what it might have been like to do such work.

3 Use the evidence on this page to fill in questionnaire **I** about life in a coalmine.

- **a** How did the following die?
  John Roberts
  James Harvey
  Richard Pritchard
  Richard Sheppard
- **b** Who was Betty Harris?
  Where did she work?
  What did working as a drawer mean?
  What were conditions like for workers in her mine?
  What hours did she work?
- **c** How was coal transported in the mine?
- **d** How did miners get the coal out of the coal seam?

4 Write a story about a day in a mine in which there was an explosion at the coal face.

5 If you wanted to find out more about conditions in mines in the 1840s, how would you go about it?

6 How useful are **A**, **C** and **F**, and **B** and **D** as historical sources?

FACTORY AND MINE REFORM

Has the cane been banned in your school? If you have a job, does your boss ever hit you? What hours each week do you and your friends work?

A hundred and fifty years ago many children of your age had full-time jobs. Let us go back to August 1832 to find out what children's working conditions were like. The scene is a room in the House of Commons, Westminster. A group of MPs is hearing evidence about how employers treat children who work in cotton factories. One of the MPs, Michael Sadler, asks Mark Best, an overseer, about straps used to flog factory children.

B

4.00 am	Get up
6.00 am	Start work
8.00 am	Breakfast
8.30 am	Back to work
12 noon	Stop for lunch
2.00 pm	Afternoon work starts
7.30 pm	Stop work for evening
8.00 pm	Go to bed

A Mark Best *They are about a foot and a half long, and there is a stick at the end, and the end they beat with is cut in the direction of my fingers, thus, having five or six thongs . . . Some of them are set in a handle, some are not.*

Michael Sadler *You say you had one of these delivered to you by the master, who urged you to make use of it, and to lay it on freely?*

Mark Best *Yes.*

Michael Carter *Do you think you could have got the quantity of work out of the children for*

D

so great a number of hours (from 6 am to 7 pm or 5 am to 9 pm) *without that cruel treatment?*

Mark Best *For that number of hours, I could not, I think; it is a long time. The speed of the machinery is calculated and they know how much work it will do, and unless they are driven and flogged up, they cannot get the work they want from them.*

Mark Best's evidence was typical. **B** gives an idea of the hours a child worked. What was it like to work in Mark Best's factory? Joseph Hebergam, aged 17, had worked for ten years in a spinning factory like the one on pages 38-39. He had to crawl under unguarded machinery. Joseph told Michael Sadler:

C *When I had worked about half a year, a weakness fell into my knees and ankles; it continued, and it has got worse. In the morning I could hardly walk, and my brother and sister used out of kindness to take me under each arm, and run with me, a good mile, to the mill, and my legs dragged on the ground in consequence of the pain; I could not talk. If we were five minutes too late the overlooker would take a strap and beat us till we were black and blue.*

Michael Sadler's committee of MPs wrote a report about what they discovered. In 1833 an Act of Parliament tried to end the worst of the horrors in the textile factories.

E

Year	Measure	What it Did
1842	Mines Act	Women, girls and boys under the age of ten not to work in mines. Inspectors to report on mines.
1844	Factory Act	Children from 8—13 restricted to half time working—6½ hours—before or after noon.
1847	Factory Act	People under 18 and all women only to work ten hours in one day.
1867	Factory Act	Brought most industries under the control of the Factory Acts.
1878	Workshop Regulation Act	Brought small workshops and work at home under control of Factory Acts.

Children and adults still worked in foul conditions in most industries. The government set up other enquiries into work in factories and mines. **D** is evidence from the 1842 report on coal mines. In 1842 Parliament passed a Mines Act, and in 1844 a second Factory Act. The factory reformers managed to pass another Factory Act in 1847. It cut working hours to ten hours a day for women and children. In the 1860s more Acts were passed to cover most other industries, and in 1878 a single Act was passed to take in all industries. **E** shows what these Acts did.

??????????????????????????

1 Use **A** to draw a picture of an overseer's strap. What do you think it would have been like to have been beaten by one? Why were they used in factories?

2 Make a diary entry for a day in the life of a factory worker in a cotton mill who was your age in 1830. Talk about:

getting up; going to work; starting work; the overseer; the scene inside the factory; working the machines; events in the day; meal times; going home; bedtime.

3 At what date, and how, were the following child workers helped by an Act of Parliament:

miners; lace workers; slate workers; chimney sweeps; cotton workers; domestic servants?

4 Use the evidence on these pages, and what else you can find out about, to put forward your own ideas about what laws you think should have been passed to protect children and women working in cotton factories in the 1830s.

What would you do about:

a the hours they should work;
b when they should start and stop work each day;
c the jobs they should be allowed to do;
d making machines safe;
e the kind of schooling children should have;
f setting up inspectors to make sure your Act was carried out, and what powers they should have.

THE GROWING POPULATION

A and **B** give you an idea of how the number of people in Britain grew from 1740 to 1900. This *population increase* meant that a great many more people lived in towns. From 1740 both old and new industrial centres expanded very fast—**C.**

D and **E** are maps of the same part of an old country town, Shrewsbury, in 1746 and 1832. Some of the new industrial and mining towns were planned, like **F**, Whitehaven in Cumbria, a coal mining centre and port. Many industrial centres like Birmingham and Manchester grew up without any planning.

??????????????

1 What does the following evidence tell us about the growth of the industrial town from 1740 to 1900? The numbers refer to the piece of evidence indicated.

a 1 – 5 in **E;**
b 6 – 12 in **F.**
(*clues—coal mines, workers' homes, warehouses, churches, the port.*)

2 Imagine you were visiting the area shown in **D** and **E** in 1746 and 1832. Say how things had changed at points 1, 2, 3, 4 and 5 between these dates.

A **Population in 1740**

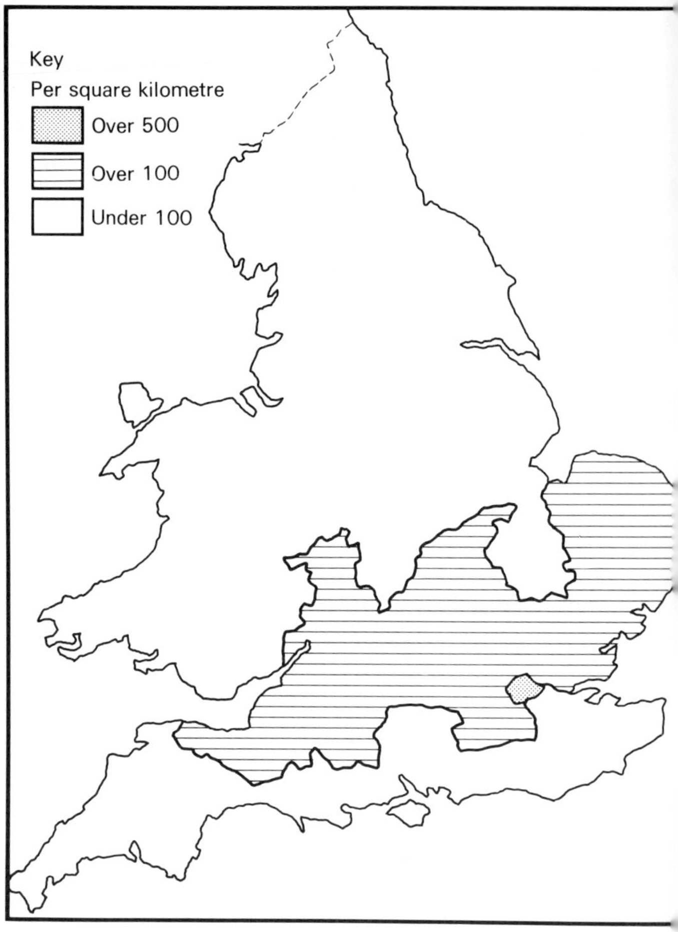

B **Population in 1900**

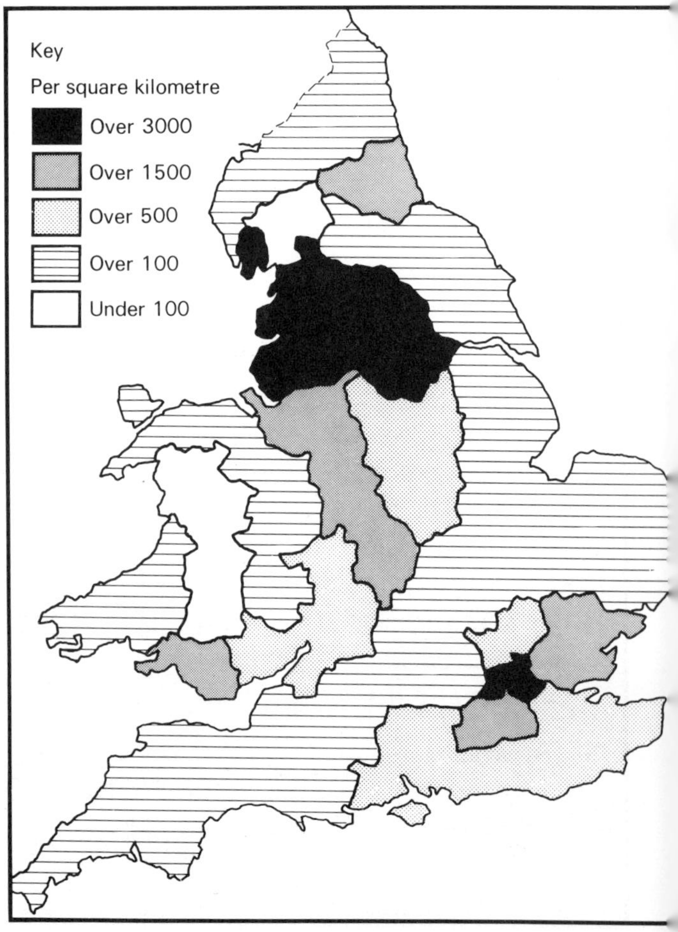

C

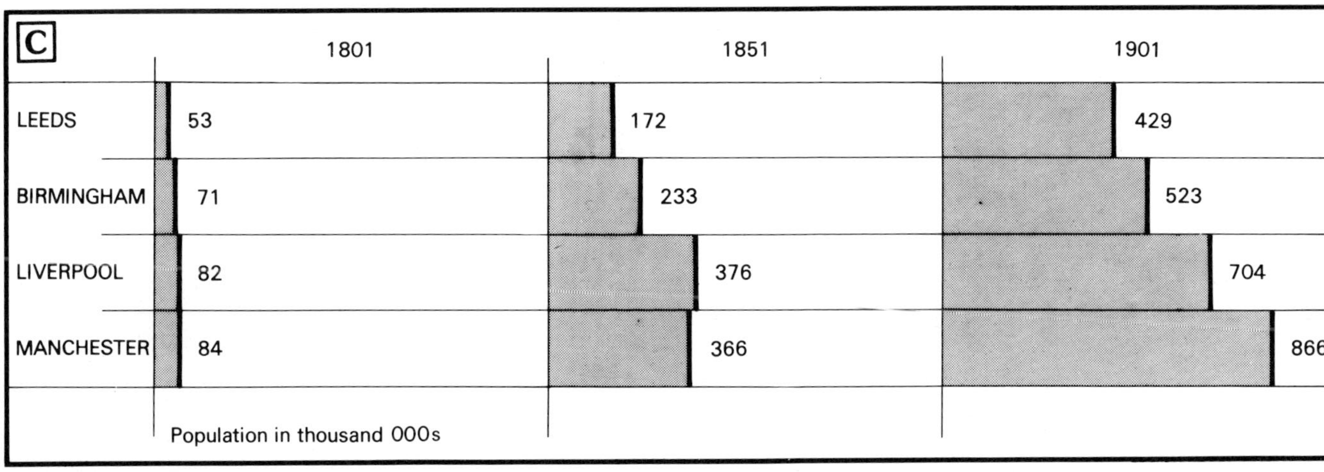
1801
1851
1901
LEEDS 53 172 429
BIRMINGHAM 71 233 523
LIVERPOOL 82 376 704
MANCHESTER 84 366 866
Population in thousand 000s

D

This PLAN of SHREWSBURY
J. Rocque.
CASTLE HILL
SEVERN

E

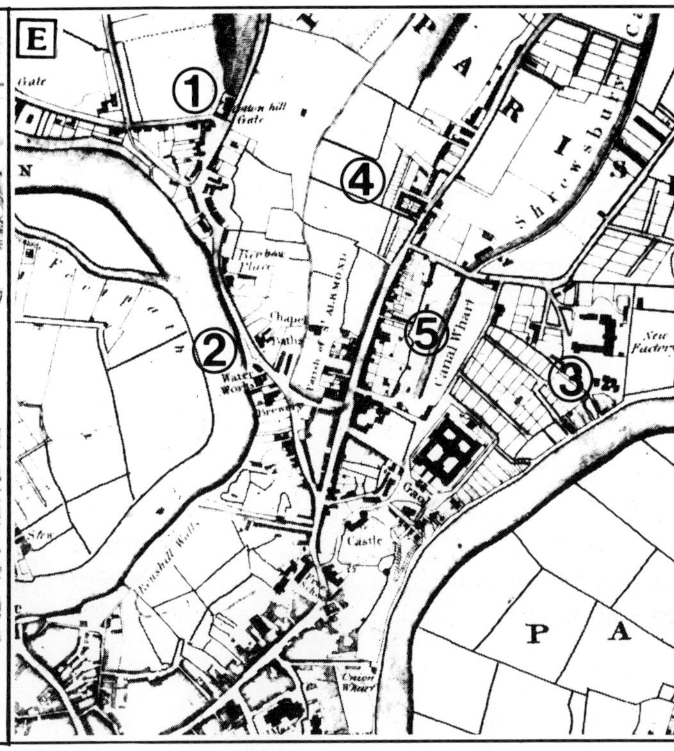
1
2
3
4
5
Canal Wharf
Castle
P A

F

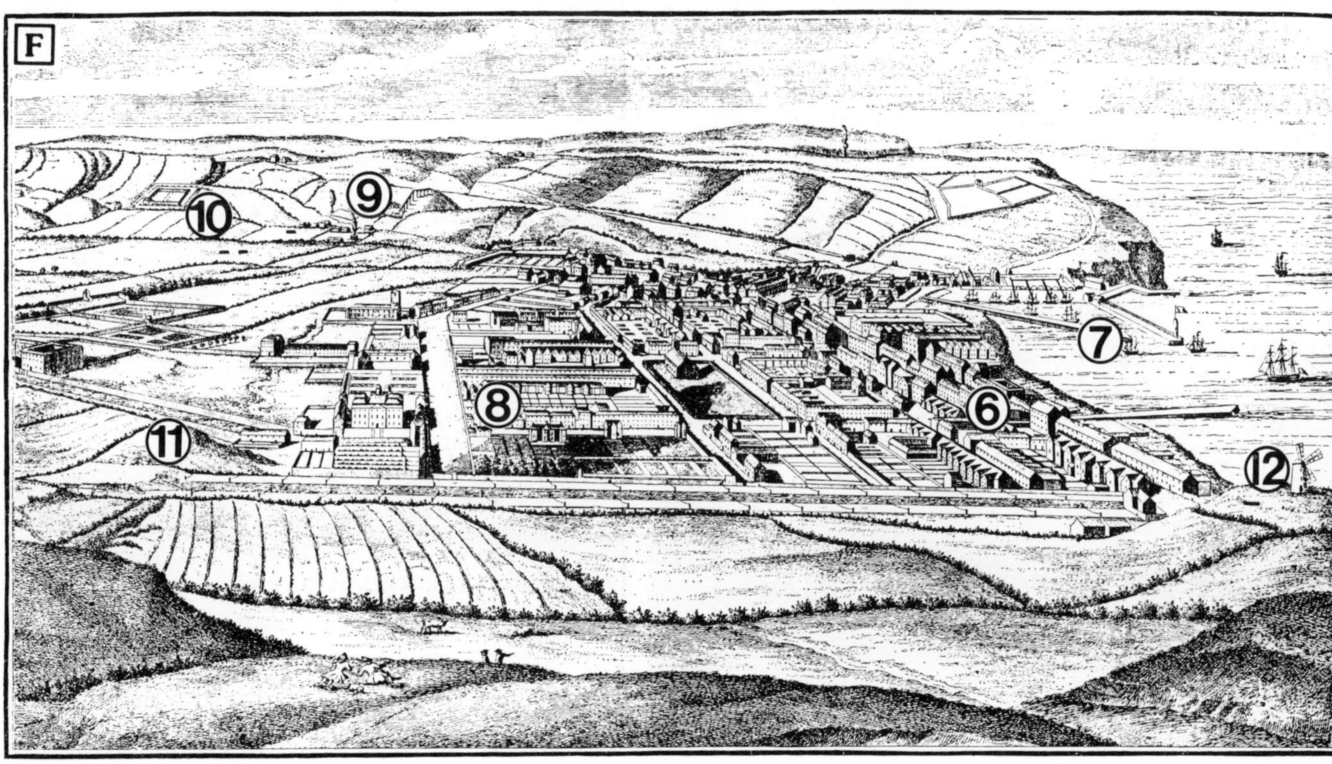
6
7
8
9
10
11
12

THE INDUSTRIAL CITY

B

C

The largest cotton city was Manchester (see pages 40-41 **F,** 54-55 **C**) In 1832 a Dr Kay wrote about it.

A *The greatest portion of those districts lived in by the labouring population (mill workers) are newly built. . . . The houses are ill drained, often ill ventilated, unprovided with toilets, and in consequence, the streets which are narrow, unpaved and worn into deep ruts, become the common resting place of mud, refuse and disgusting rubbish . . . In Parliament Street there is only one toilet for 380 inhabitants, which is placed in a narrow passage, from where its flow of muck infests the close-by houses, and must prove a most fertile source of disease.*

B is a view of Manchester in the 1860s. **C** is a photograph of a typical worker's house, and **D** a plan of one. What was life like in these houses? In 1835 a government report on Manchester's cotton factories said of a better-off cotton worker's family:

E *Breakfast is generally porridge, bread and milk, lined with flour or oatmeal. On Sunday, a cup of tea and bread and butter. Dinner, on week days, potatoes and bacon, and bread, which is generally white. On a Sunday, a little* *flesh meat; no butter, egg, or pudding. Teatime, every day, tea and bread and butter; nothing extra on Sunday at tea. Supper, oatmeal, porridge and milk; sometimes potatoes and milk. Sundays, sometimes a little bread and cheese for supper; never have this on weekdays. Now and then buys eggs when they are as low as a halfpenny apiece, and fries them to bacon. They never taste any other vegetables than potatoes; never use any beer or spirits.*

They subscribe a penny a week for each child to a funeral society. . . Two of the children go to school at 3d (1½p) a week each. They are taught reading for this, but not writing. Have a few books, such as a Bible, hymn book, and several small books that the children have got as prizes at the Sunday school.

D

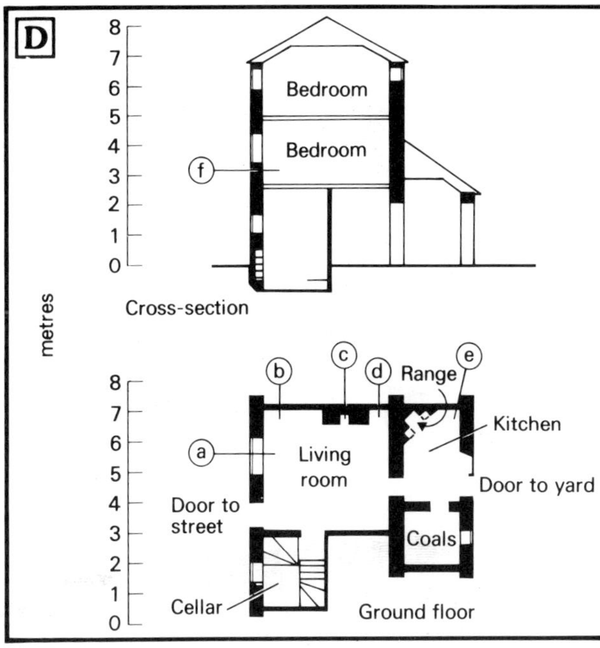

E is a page from the 1842 government report on factory conditions (see pages 50-51). It gives you more evidence about life in the new industrial cities.

F

EMPLOYMENT OF CHILDREN. 91

The fifth family visited consisted of a man, his wife, and six children:

A Spinner.

Earnings.	£.	*s.*	*d.*	Expenditure.	£.	*s.*	*d.*
1st, boy, aged 15, feeder . . .	0	6	0	Flour	0	9	0
2nd „ „ 14, piecer . . .	0	4	0	Meal	0	1	0
3rd „ „ 12 „ . . .	0	2	0	Yeast	0	0	8
4th, girl „ 10, cardsetter . .	0	0	6	Soap	0	1	0
5th „ „ 7 „ . .	0	0	0	Butter	0	2	0
6th „ „ 5 „ . .	0	0	0	Candles	0	1	0
Self, wife assisting	0	18	0	Meat	0	4	6
				Cheese	0	1	0
				Sugar	0	2	0
				Potatoes	0	1	6
				Coals	0	2	0
				Tea or coffee	0	0	10
				Worsted, &c.	0	0	4
				Rent	0	1	9
				Balance	0	1	11
	1	10	6		1	10	6

This house consists of two rooms and pantry. In the lower room stood two good clean al tables, a good cupboard with drawers, a neat painted chest of drawers, shelves, with plates, ives, and forks, a large oak chest, eight chairs, window-curtains, five pictures framed, poker, ngs, clean blackleaded grate.

In the room above stood four bedsteads, four good flock-beds, a counterpane and two ankets on each, with bolster, pillow, and cases: everything remarkably clean and wholeme. On the window I observed two Bibles, Prayer-book, Pilgrim's Progress, and four ymn-books. Four out of the six children could read, but none write.

The wife brews small ale once a-fortnight if the balance of accounts will admit of it. All tend a place of worship on Sunday.

Sixth family visited consists of a man, his wife, and six children:

Spinner.

Earnings.	£.	*s.*	*d.*	Expenditure.	£.	*s.*	*d.*
1st, girl, aged 16, feeder . . .	0	6	0	Flour	0	9	0
2nd „ „ 14, piecer . . .	0	4	6	Oatmeal	0	4	0
3rd „ „ 11, winder . . .	0	2	0	Yeast	0	0	8
4th, boy „ 9	0	0	0	Potatoes	0	1	6
5th „ „ 7	0	0	0	Meat	0	2	4
6th, girl „ 5	0	0	0	Tea	0	0	6
Self, wife assisting	1	0	0	Sugar	0	1	0
				Coffee	0	0	6
				Soap	0	1	0
				Butter	0	0	6
				Beer	0	1	1½
				Thread, &c.	0	0	4
				Coals	0	1	6
				Rent	0	2	0
				Balance	0	6	6½
	1	12	6		1	12	6

This is another wretched house of two rooms. The first having a deal table, broken chairs, d old bedstead, flock-bed and pillow, a rotten blanket and quilt, a few odd cups and saucers, d porridge basins, a corner cupboard minus everything.

In the room above two broken bedsteads, a box, inverted tub, dirty chaff-beds and old ankets.

The wife remarked,—" My daughters wish to appear at church as other girls, but my husnd drinks so much that I can only now and then get anything from him when in work; t now he is so short of work that we are pined (starved), besides he grudges the girls anying to appear decent in.

? ? ? ? ? ? ? ? ? ? ? ?

1 What would it have been like to visit Manchester in 1832, and have gone around a cotton worker's house? Say what you would have seen, heard and smelt:

—going along the city's roads;

—in Parliament Street;

—passing factories.

What might you have seen in the cotton worker's house at the following points at breakfast time—**a, b, c, d, e, f**?

2 Draw up a table comparing your life at home with the life of one of the families in **F.**

3 How has life in an industrial city changed since the 1830s?

THE GREAT DEPRESSION 1873-96

A *There is no main industry carried on in York. The North Eastern Railway Company finds employment in York for about 5500 men and lads, but whether they work as joiners, fitters, bricklayers, painters, labourers, their wages are fixed by the wages which obtain for each trade. . . . There are also between two and three thousand persons employed in cocoa and confectionery* (sweets) *works. In addition to the above there are a number of industries employing fewer people, such as flour-milling, brewing etc.*

York was like many other towns in 1899, when **A** was written. How might the Great Depression in industry, which lasted from 1873 to 1896, have affected it? **B, C, D, E** and **F** are graphs of what happened to cotton and wool cloth making, coal mining and iron and steel manufacturing from 1873-96. In which years do you think the depression in these industries was at its worst?

The government was very worried about the depression in the main industries of the *First Industrial Revolution*—wool and cotton, coal, and iron and steel.

How did firms manage in these hard times? A firm of engineers, Matheson and Grant, wrote a report about engineering's problems in 1886:

G *The year just closed has been one of the worst ever in the engineering trades.*

Decline in old industries meant fall in prices and wages. This caused trouble, and there were strikes. At the same time new kinds of industries were starting—chemicals, electricity and gas. **J** lists the ten most important industries in 1907.

B

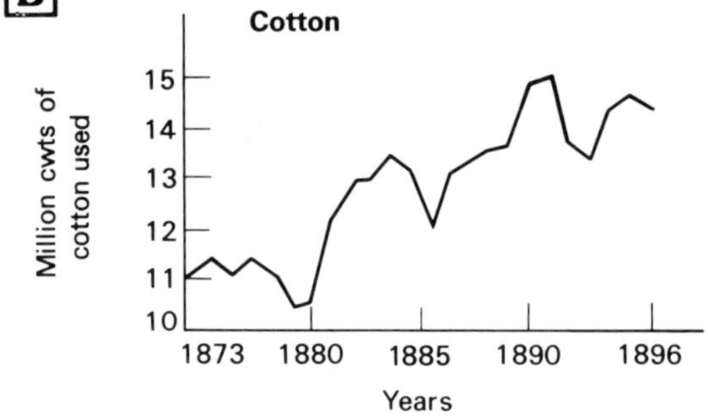

C

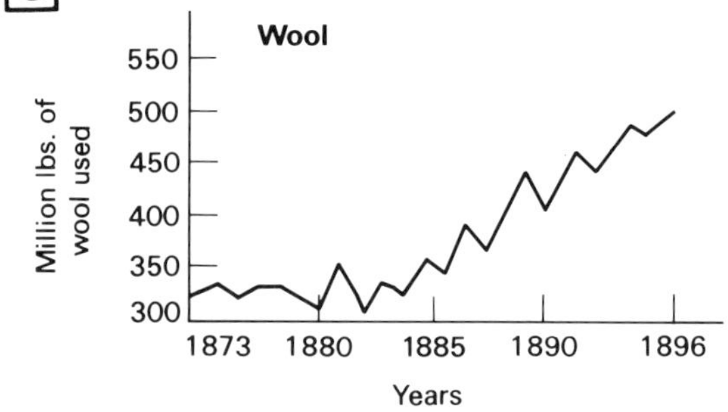

D

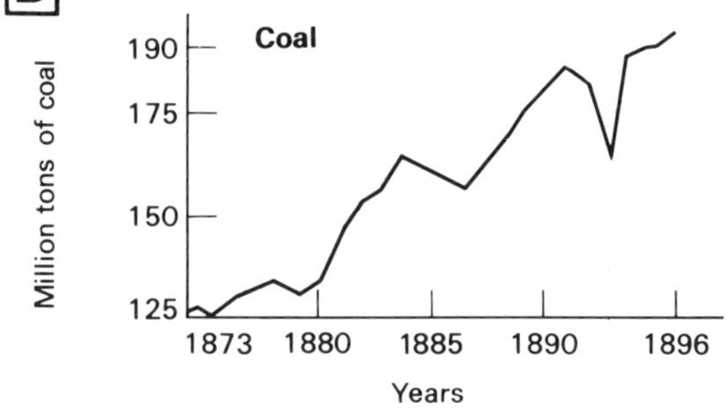

E

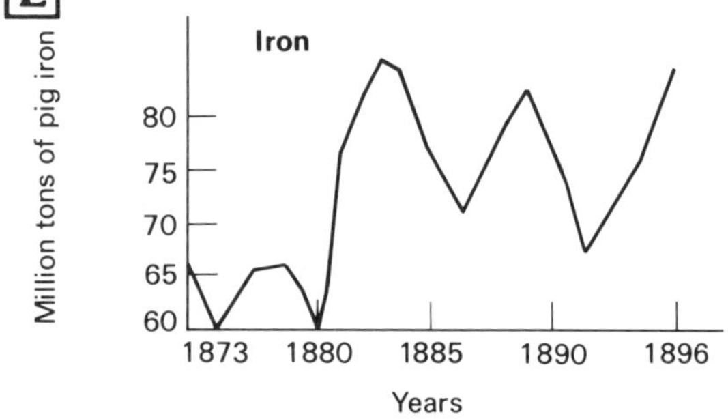

F

J

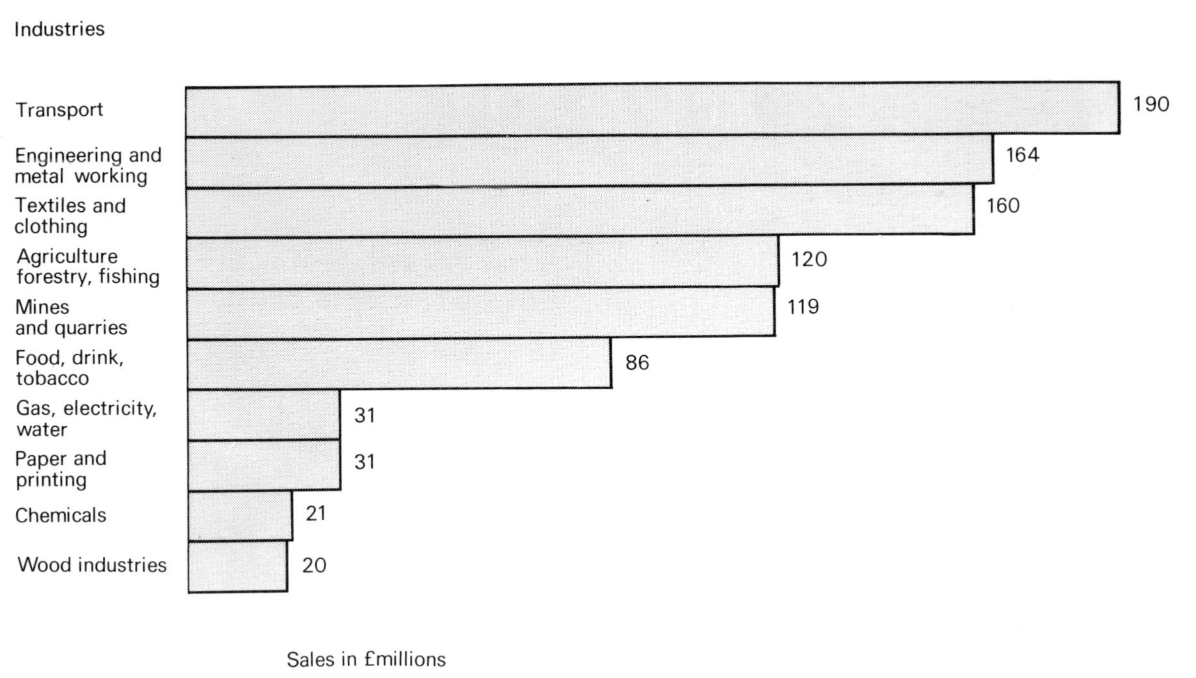

H

In several branches a slight improvement has set in which is likely to continue. The prospects for the coming spring are brighter than they have been for the last two years. Since our July report there have been large investments of capital money in work which gives employment to engineers, and an increasing expenditure among firms may be looked for.

The revival of railway building in the United States has given great impetus to the iron and steel trades of that country, and though free trade with Great Britain is not allowed, the close links between the two countries has always led to a corresponding improvement.

Coal has been cheaper than ever during the last year. . . . Iron: the continued fall in the prices of pig iron during the first half of 1886 was stopped. The prices of rolled iron have gone up and down during the last six months, they are now slightly higher than during the summer. They would be still higher but for the competition of steel, not only in shipbuilding, but in boilers, bridges and other structures.

1 Find the answer to each question in the piece of evidence listed by it.

a When was the depression at its worst in: cotton (**B**), wool (**C**), coal (**D**) and iron (**E**)?

b Was it worse in iron than steel (**E, F**)?

c What new industries grew during the depression—**J**?

2 If you had visited York in 1890, say how the depression might have affected people who worked on the railways, in sweet making, brewing and flour milling.

3 How did Matheson and Grant think that the depression in engineering might end? Read the rest of their report in **H,** and mention:

investment; railways; coal prices; cheap iron; steel.

4 What form did the Great Depression in industry take from 1873-96?

THE AGRICULTURAL DEPRESSION, 1873-96

Mr Prout (see page 13) was asked:

A *May I ask if you have been able to farm profitably during the late trying seasons?*

In the year 1879, I lost £500.

Why had this happened? From 1873 to 1896 British farming went into a decline—the *Agricultural Depression.* Worst hit were growers of wheat, although from 1878-80 the raising of animals made very little money, too.

An 1881 Royal Commission looked at the reasons for the depression. A government official, Mr Coleman, made a report on farming in Yorkshire. One of the farms he looked at was Mr Walter Strickney's, of 1 200 acres. The land was mainly clay. The prices of his wheat and barley fell sharply from 1868-79. Mr Strickney said the reasons for the depression were:

B

a *First and foremost to a succession of bad seasons ending in the bad harvest of 1879.*

b *Undue restrictions as to conditions of farming.*

c *Land let since 1868 has been generally let at too high a rent to meet bad seasons.*

d *Prices are generally held down by American imports, by poverty and bad trade in industry,* (see The Great Depression, pages 58-59), *and also owing to the poor quality of home-grown crops.*

e *The rates have increased lately. . .*

C is more evidence about the agricultural depression. A major cause was the import of cheap grain from America. Railways and steamships made it easy to import lots of cheaply grown wheat from the prairies. Sheep and cattle disease also hit the animal farmers badly in 1878-80.

C **The price of wheat**

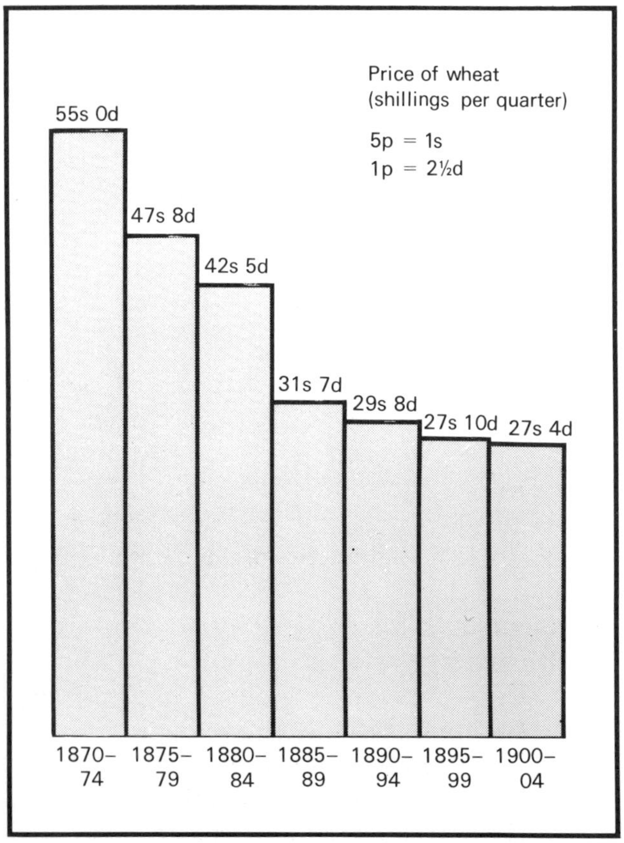

1 Draw up a list of points to show why Mr Prout's farm lost money in 1879. Mention the following:

a bad weather
b rents
c price of wheat and oats
d payment of rates
e cattle and sheep disease

2 Use the evidence on this page, and what else you can find, to write a history of the Agricultural Depression.

FARMING TRANSFORMED, 1740-1900

Map **A** is of Area 2 on page 7. It shows the region around the growing industrial town of Molesbury. In 1740 10 000 people lived in Molesbury, in 1850 80 000 and in 1900 160 000. Workers live in houses built round the many factories. Each square on **A** is of a farming area, and represents one main kind of farming, for example sheep grazing. How would you expect each piece of land to be used in 1740, 1850 and 1900? Use the notes to help you.

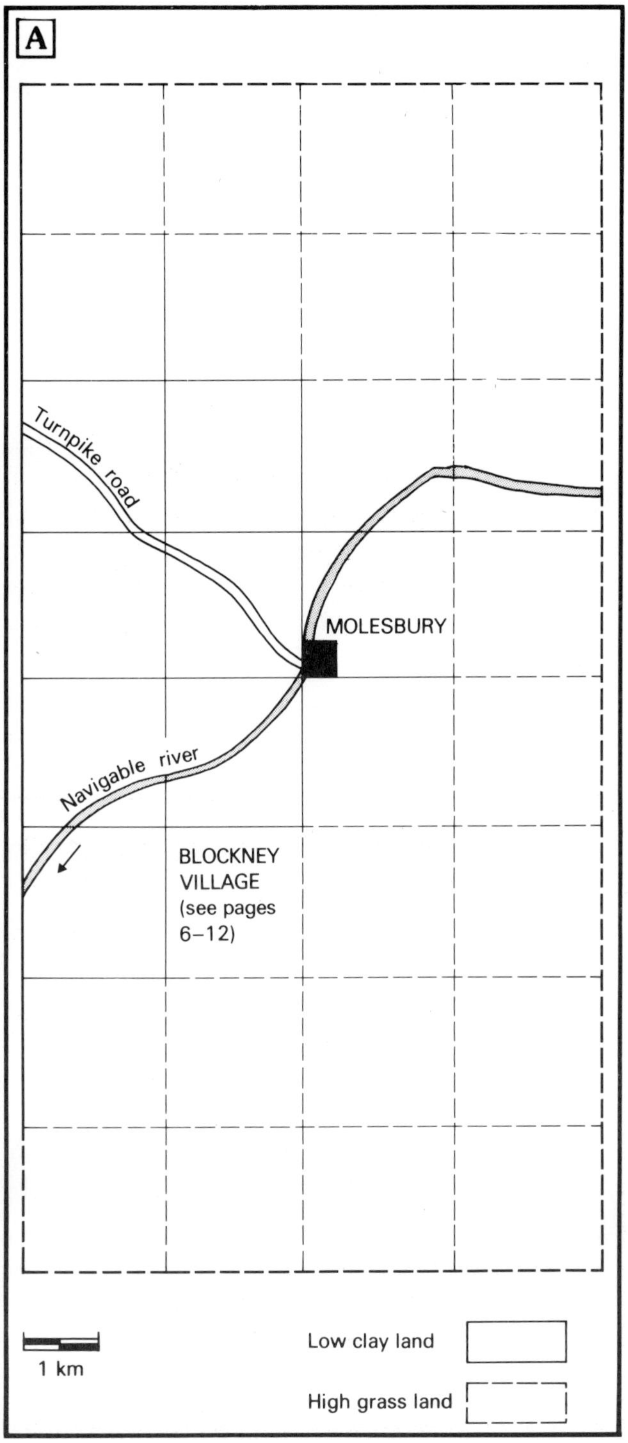

1740

Notes Molesbury is a small farming town of 10 000 people. The area is still farmed in the old way, although one area has gone over to the Norfolk rotation.

Areas Unused high land (*8 squares*)
Highland sheep grazing (*8 squares*)
Open fields—normal three-field pattern (see *The Normans*, pages 33, 36) (*15 squares*)
Enclosed farming—wheat, barley, turnips, clover in rotation (*1 square*)

1850

Notes Molesbury has been *industrialised.* There are cotton spinning and weaving mills and a large iron works. The town now has a population of 80 000, all of whom eat food which comes from the farms round the town. A network of turnpike roads and railways runs out into the countryside. Farmers can easily get their crops and animals to the town's markets and corn mills.

Areas Highland sheep grazing (*8 squares*)
Upland cattle grazing (*4 squares*)
Cattle rearing in low-lying areas (*3 squares*)
Enclosed farming (11 squares)
Dairy farming (*3 squares*)
Market gardening (*2 squares*)
Housing and industry (*1 square*)

1900

Notes Molesbury has gone on growing. There are new chemical and electrical factories in the town, although there has been a decline in cotton spinning and weaving. The town's population has reached 160 000. The demand for food is greater. Farmers have been badly hit by the imports of cheap wheat from America.

Areas Highland sheep grazing (*10 squares*)
Upland cattle grazing (*5 squares*)
Cattle rearing in low-lying areas (*6 squares*)
Enclosed farming (*4 squares*)
Dairy farming (*3 squares*)
Market gardening (*3 squares*)
Housing and industry (*1 square*)

TRADE, 1740-1900

A

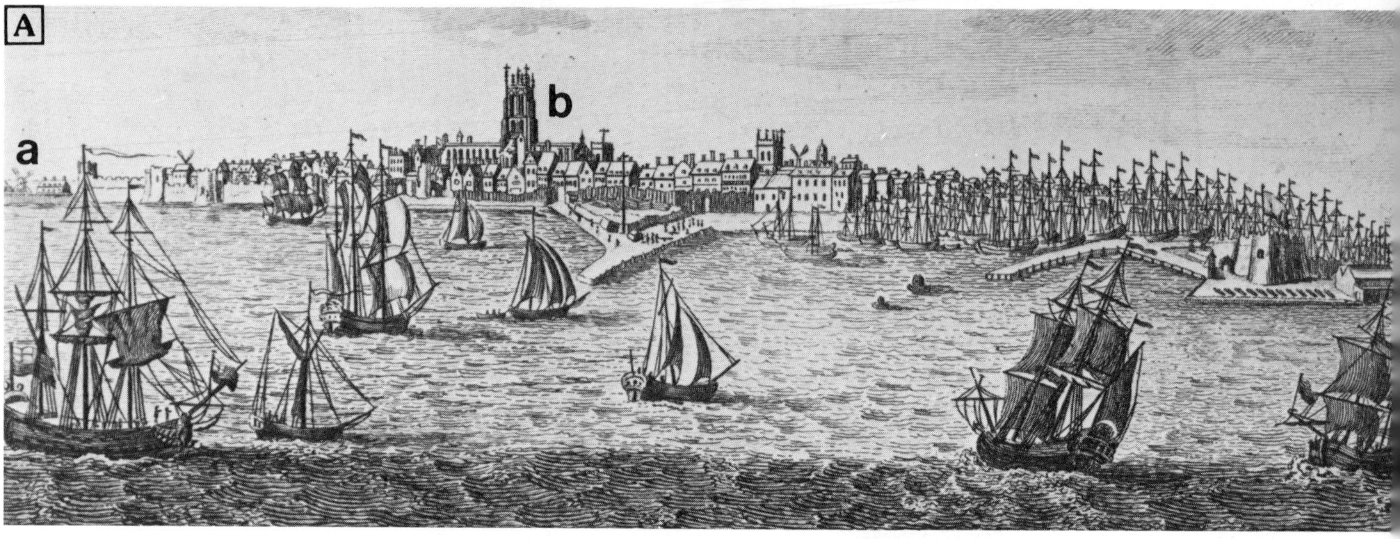

C **Britain's world trade routes in 1740**

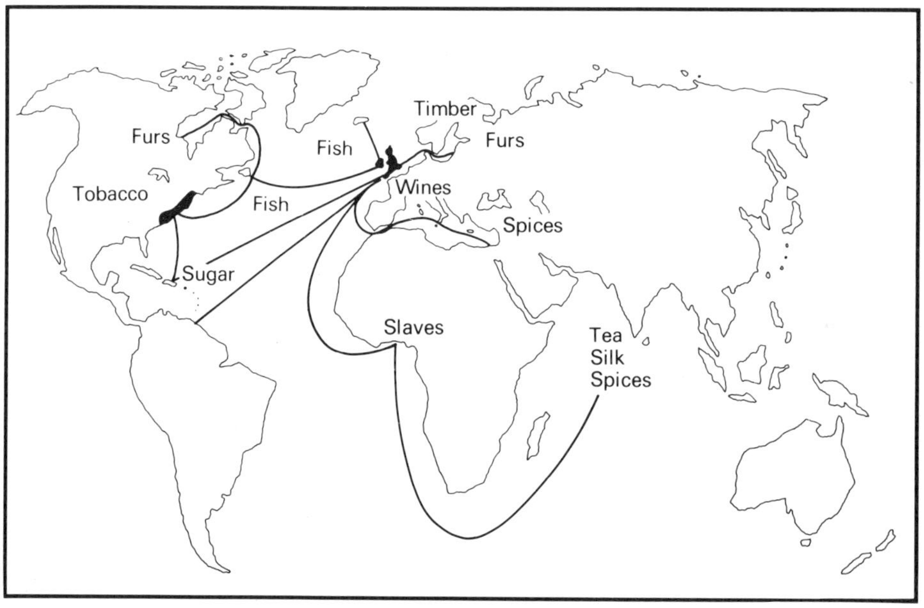

D **Britain's world trade routes in 1900**

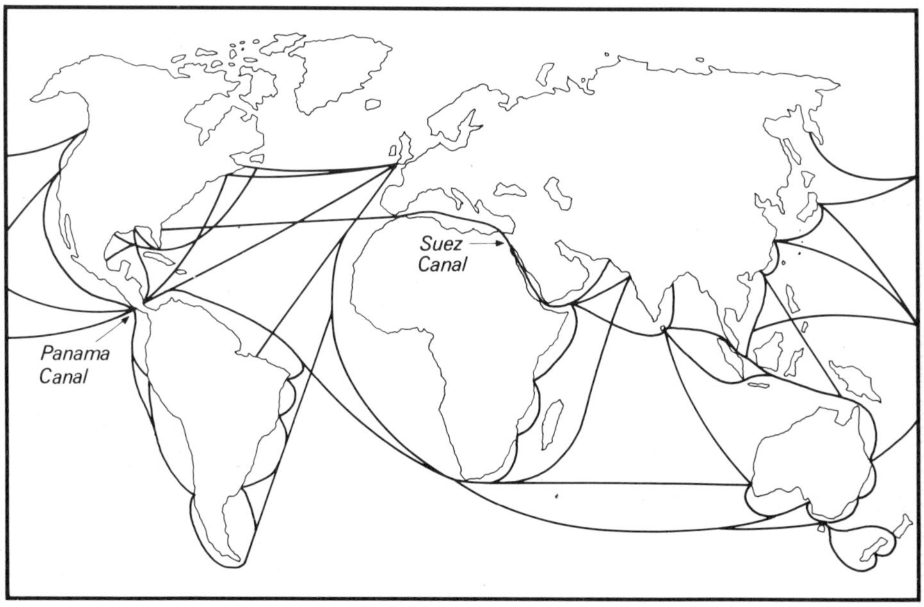

If you had stood at the dockside of Newcastle on Tyne in 1740, you would have seen a view like **A**. Around 150 years later it would have looked like **B**. There were many reasons for these changes:

a The *Transport Revolution* affected ships. In 1740 ships were built of wood and used wind power for their sails. In 1900 most ships were built of iron and used engines which ran on steam power. Ships were also much bigger.

b The *Industrial Revolution* meant that traders had many more goods to sell abroad.

c *New markets* had been found and developed throughout the world—**C** and **D**.

How did these changes affect ports like Newcastle? **E** shows the import trade of the port in 1844. **F** shows the growth of British trade from 1740-1900.

B

E **Imports to the port of Newcastle upon Tyne in 1744**

	Africa	Belgium	Canada	Denmark	East Indies	France	Germany	Holland	Italy	Jersey	Norway	Portugal	Russia	S. America	Spain	Sweden	Turkey	United States
Number of ships	8	7	46	109	4	37	178	64	20	5	77	8	60	3	9	28	4	1
Apples and pears			•			•		•										
Beef and pork				•			•						•					
Bark		•					•	•	•		•					•		
Bones							•	•			•					•		
Cheese								•										
Currants, grapes																	•	
Flax, hemp							•						•					
Grain				•			•	•			•		•			•	•	
Grease				•			•	•			•		•			•		
Guano	•													•				
Hides, horses, hoofs	•			•			•	•					•	•				
Linseed	•				•		•				•		•				•	
Mats		•		•		•	•	•			•		•			•		
Nuts									•									
Oil cake				•			•	•			•					•		
Onions						•	•	•				•						
Oranges									•	•		•						
Rope							•				•		•			•		
Sealskins							•											
Spirits				•			•	•										
Sugar					•													
Timber	•				•		•				•		•			•		
Wine						•	•	•	•	•	•	•			•	•		

F

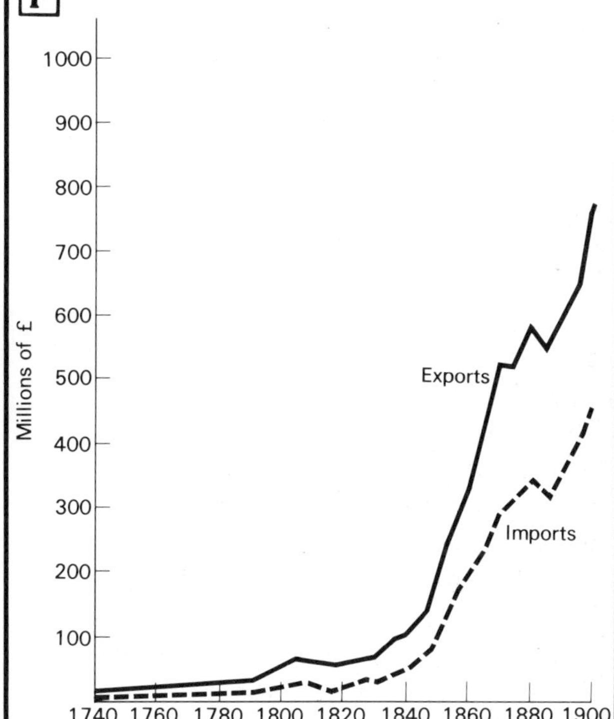

? ?

1 How and why had things changed at the dockside between 1740 and 1900? Mention what you can see at points **a, b, c, d, e, f.**

2 Mark on map **D** where a Newcastle merchant in 1844 would have got the following goods:
sugar; whale fins; nuts; guano (bird muck); apples; turpentine; hemp; grapes.

3 How many of the goods imported in 1844 might not have been imported in 1740?

4 Explain why British trade expanded so much between 1740 and 1900.

DEVELOPING BRITAIN: MAP

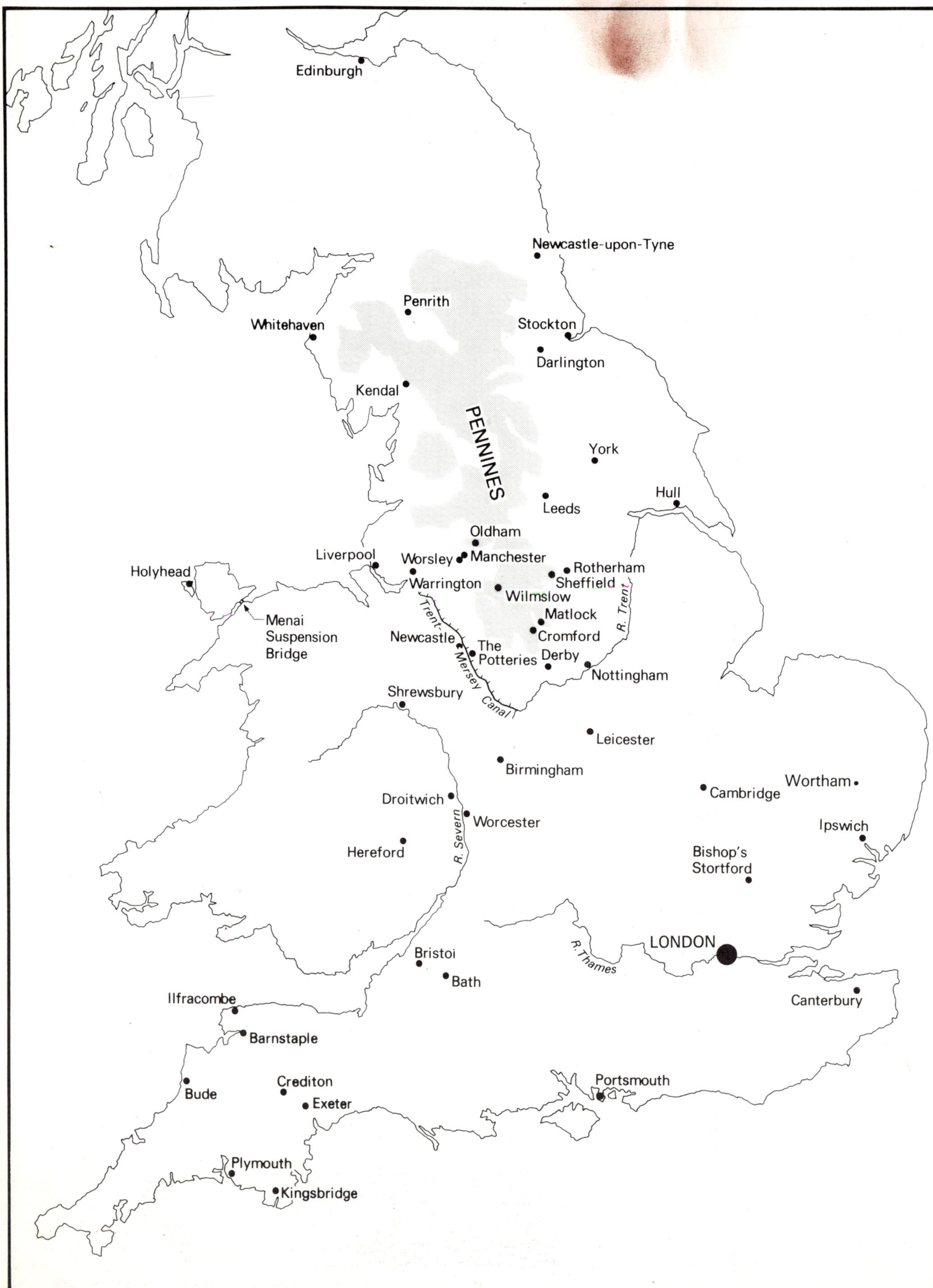